Aurélie & Max

Bob Sennett

Copyright © 2025 by Bob Sennett.

Bob Sennett asserts the moral right to be identified as the author of this work.

Artwork: Eugène Atget (public domain).

Cover designed by Spectrum Books.

ISBN: 978-1-915905-58-1

All rights reserved. No part of this book may be used or reproduced, transmitted, downloaded, decompiled, reverse engineered or stored in or introduced into any information storage and retrieval system, in any form or by any means without the express written permission of the author or of Spectrum Books, except for brief quotations used for promotion or in reviews.

This book is a work of fiction. The names, characters, places, and incidents portrayed in it are the work of the author's imagination. Any resemblance to actual persons, living or dead, or events, is entirely coincidental..

First Edition, Spectrum Books, 2025

Discover more books at www.spectrum-books.com

To John, as always...

I

Marc & Sarah

Even in the heart of the winter of 1919, when the Seine was glazed with ice and windows were kept tightly shut, Dr. Marcus Greenspan found it easy to believe in a warm and shining future. The Great War had ended; the world would spin again, and it was just possible that a man could dream and never need to wake.

Evidence of the conflagration had not disappeared; that was why Marc was still in France. There were men in shock, men missing limbs, men as lost as shooting stars. Still, it was a far cry from the screaming shells, the skies black with smoke, and the insufficient, blood-soaked tourniquets of the days gone by. Compared to No Man's Land, the American Hospital in Paris was a resort.

Marc spent every day but Sunday there; his specialty was surgery, but he volunteered for anything that was necessary from setting broken limbs to serving lunch. For the duration, it was the best way Marc knew how to help, and hardly less so now, for the so-called peace.

Paris was for the moment the center of the universe. With the start of the international conference, the crowds in the streets had thickened as the diplomats and secretaries and reporters flooded into the city; that morning, it took Marc longer than usual to get from his flat in Clichy to the hospital. He also needed to stop along the way to check his box in the post office; it had been five days since he last looked.

There was a letter from Sarah.

25 Dec. 1918

Mon cher,

You see, I am practicing my French. Mama thinks it still might be ages before I get 'over there,' but I tell her the spring is not so far away, and of course I keep praying that you will come home before then. It's Christmas Day, and I miss you so, my darling! I hope despite everything you managed a lovely holiday amongst your men; it was a peaceful one, I suppose, at last. I know you are quite busy, but I still run out to our mailbox every day to look for news from you.

Father came down with a bit of the croup last week, but it seems we have so far dodged the flu. The Johnsons have not been as lucky; Mary's mother passed away, and the funeral was dreadful. I shudder to think of you under your circumstances. But enough morbidity; life is too short as it is to dwell on endings, especially when for you and me there is so much of the future to consider.

I can well afford the extra postage for a second page, but what else is there to say but 'come home, come home, come home?'

With love from your devoted friend, Sarah.

Marc tried to remember the last time he wrote—it was likely sometime around Thanksgiving, certainly after the Armistice was signed. Louisville seemed so far away, in time as much as in distance. He'd been in Europe for nearly three years; how had it all passed by so quickly? Wasn't it only a moment ago he was standing on the dock in New York, waving goodbye to the anonymous crowd?

Marcus Greenspan and Sarah Gold had been engaged since the spring of '14, before either one of them had ever imagined being separated by a war. The couple believed they were destined to be married from the day they met, at a Rosh Hashanah service at their temple over a dozen years ago. Marc and Sarah were teenagers then, dutifully sitting in the cold, dark sanctuary—

Marc with his father below, Sarah with her mother above. There was a small reception in the overheated vestibule after the ceremony. The rabbi introduced Philip Greenspan to Josiah Gold; their two children conversed and discovered they held common likes and interests.

Without brothers or sisters for company, the young Mr. Greenspan and the slightly younger Miss Gold naturally became friends, although not, at first, intimate ones. Their friendship blossomed into something resembling love, and when the time came for Marc to head off to Harvard and earn first his baccalaureate and then his medical degree, he promised Sarah they would remain a couple but he left his vow vague enough for an open-ended interpretation. There was a primacy to their relations that still came up short of any kind of long-range commitment.

When Marc came back to Louisville with his education behind him and an expansive future in medicine ahead, he and Sarah began a more formal courtship. Like a slow-developing photograph, steady dates turned into a vision of a shared future. Six months later, Marc bought Sarah an engagement ring that was far too expensive for his budget; it was an act more precipitous in many ways than any he had ever previously attempted, and it made him nervous in a way he didn't completely understand.

When Europe erupted in war, his former colleagues at Harvard recruited medical volunteers. Marc had retained his idealistic streak—some called it naiveté— and jumped at the chance to serve. He quit his residency at the Louisville City Hospital. He knew his fiancé would disapprove, perhaps as much or more than his parents, but he felt something resembling a calling.

Sarah suggested they get married straight away, but Marc deferred, claiming an optimism he secretly lacked. The training took months, but his was an unswerving commitment, and by the spring of '16 he was in khakis at Verdun, bandaging up wounded French soldiers. He was twenty-five years old.

Marc imagined he'd been prepared for what he'd see and do on the front, but he discovered quite quickly that his imagination was no match for German shells or French weather. The ground was flooded in the spring and frozen in the winter, and their tents were always torn. The men that were brought to those tents had wounds that bled into the earth like unholy water and caused them to scream as much from the incomprehensibility of it as from the pain.

The first unit to which Marc was assigned lost all but five men, and two of the survivors were nearly blinded by gas. Then there was an incident one day in the early summer of '17. Marc's unit was trapped on a ridge in Passchendaele. As Marc rolled down the hill to try to reach a man whose arm had been shattered by a shell his helmet was split in half by shrapnel. One turn of his head six inches in either direction would have decapitated him. From this, Marc finally learned that staying alive was his life's only goal.

His letters to and from Sarah were Marc's only link to the world he once loved and now knew would never be the same. He had long since given up regular correspondence with his mother and father once Sarah made it clear she shared every scrap of information with them with the regularity of a diplomat; if there was ever real news, a telegram would suffice.

All the while, the good doctor Greenspan chronicled the change from innocence to experience as much within his mind as he did upon the ink-filled page, loosening his ties to Kentucky and Cambridge and the New World in a bumbling manner not unlike the way a boy untangles the string of a kite, with skips and starts that require a fundament of patience before the letting go.

Slowly but inexorably, the life he knew before the fighting began took on the faded appearance of an old photograph, while the life he was determined to live lay before him in the vivid colors of a dream. A few years may have passed on the calendar since he arrived, but ten times as many were etched into his brow and impounded in his heart.

Marc was determined to stay on to the end, and he did. For the first time in his life, he felt like he had a purpose. When peace came, his life entered a phrase that might be pleasantly labeled 'routine': walk to the hospital, check the board for his assignments, confer with his fellow doctors, share a sandwich, do his rounds, and walk home.

His social engagements were picking up and his diversions increased—there was even time for long dinners in unfamiliar neighborhoods and nights out in the clubs of Montmartre and Saint-Germain—but his sense of a mission remained unabated. The main thing now was that his life was no longer in danger for it, and his thoughts of Sarah and home—thoughts he had tried to defer for years—began to bubble up to the surface.

Marc's closest colleague at the American Hospital was Paul Cordette. Paul was British; he signed up with the declaration of war in the summer of '14 and had been in and out of France ever since. There were brief leaves for Christmas and a relatively peaceful interval in the summer of '16 when Paul was assigned to a recovery ward in Calais.

But that autumn Paul ended up trapped in the trenches of Ypres for the worst of it, and every man consigned their prayers to a dustbin. When the gas clouds parted and the smoke cleared, the soldiers discovered their prayers were answered. The battle ended but the war moved on; all the doctors in Paul's unit were transferred back to the capital to deal with the rising number of casualties. Dr. Greenspan was amongst them.

When Marc and Paul were reassigned to Paris, Paul offered to share his room in a boarding house on the same street as the Lycée Pasteur, where the British Expeditionary Forces had set up a temporary recovery ward, and Marc accepted. At first, it was convenient to live two blocks away from the hospital, but after a year of that there was too much of the smell of blood in the room and too much shared sorrow. They decided being friends was more important than saving on rent; Paul moved to Batignolles, and Marc rented a flat on the rue du Bois in Clichy. Marc now had a ten-minute walk to the hospital, but it was ten minutes away from the bone saw and the bullet tongs, ten minutes that felt like an eternity.

On the 12th of January there was snow, and the rue du Bois was mucky with melted slush. Marc took a taxi from his apartment to the hospital; he preferred walking, but with the street in such condition the trip would have taken longer and the damp on his trouser cuffs would have trailed water on the parquet through lunch.

Along the way, he mulled over his reply to Sarah. Should he write straight away with a shortage of details to prove his attentiveness, or should he wait for some change in the affairs of men to be worth ringing and beg for Sarah's forbearance? Every time Marc wrote, he felt there was more left out than said; his life in Paris overwhelmed his memory of America. It was a never-ending game, and his consideration of the new rules for it was beginning to make his head hurt.

Marc thought of stopping at a place along the boulevard Victor Hugo for coffee and a brioche; there was nothing to eat in the flat except for a half of a roast beef sandwich he brought home from yesterday's twelve-hour shift. The cost of food had risen alarmingly in the mere weeks since the last of the fighting, and what used to cost five francs now might run to nearly double that. Marc wasn't poor—no American doctor was and being paid in dollars helped—but neither could he pretend the money was endless. He got a cup of coffee at an open stand on the corner in front of the hospital and skipped the brioche.

When Marc first came over, his situation was dicey. He was a volunteer and had no salary. Many of his Ivy League colleagues were the sons of wealthy men looking for adventure; they didn't need to worry about the cost of their next meal. But Marc paid his way through Harvard with odd jobs and scholarships, and his parents could only help him out so much. He depended on the fifty dollars a month offered to him by the American Field Service, an amount that was insufficient from the beginning and by the end of the year barely covered his rent and the cost of bread and eggs. Then the United States declared war on the Central Powers, and all the American doctors who had volunteered were added to the hospital's staff and, even better, were paid a decent salary for it.

The American Hospital was relatively new—barely a decade old when Marc arrived—but the war had worn down the shiny surfaces and left something resembling a permanent gray buffer along the endless halls and long wards. At first, all the patients were lumped together—French, British, Americans, even German prisoners-of-war—and no differentiation was made between gas cases, shell shock, and broken limbs. There were too many bodies and too few attendants, and it took a monumental effort from everyone involved just to keep the whole system from collapsing in chaos.

But slowly, like a delicate filigree that needs only slight teasing to hold, the staff found a way to rehabilitate their charges. Military efficiency helped; soon there were wards dedicated to specialists, and then the languages were sorted and the English-speaking doctors had one wing, and the French and German speakers had the other, trying their best to enforce an ecumenical peace. There was a separate ward for influenza patients and starting in October everyone had to wear cloth masks. Thanks to Marc's excellent education, he spoke fluent German and was deemed especially useful in that regard; many of the other doctors spoke only French and English or pretended to do so.

That morning, Marc was in charge of a section of the German ward. At one point, right around the time of the Battle of Verdun, the ward had nearly one hundred beds, all filled with prisoners. Now there were barely two dozen beds, and some of them were empty. Since the Armistice, any German soldier capable of walking unaided had long been repatriated, and those who remained were for the most part rapidly healing. It seemed to Marc to be only a matter of time before the ward would be closed. The hospital's staff would be greatly reduced, and he would be able to think about heading home.

As Marc arrived on the ward, Paul handed him a small stack of folders.

"Three new patients this morning—two amputees, and one bullet wound," he said. "I'm heading down to the canteen. Do you want anything?"

Marc thought about the missed opportunity for a brioche and measured it against the need to check on the new admissions. He decided lunch was only two hours away.

"No, thank you, Paul."

"I'll catch up with you at the end of my shift."

"Thanks."

Marc surveyed the ward. The American Expeditionary Force had been in charge of the prisoners up until November; the latest arrangement was for the hospital to treat and repatriate as many captured men as possible. These men would then be the responsibility of the Germans, of course under the watchful eye of the occupying troops.

Marc had met, and treated, most of the men currently under care at one point or another. Many of them, the lucky ones, weren't around long enough for Marc to learn much about them except their names and their condition. During the heart of the war, when Marc's life was often in as much peril as the corps, there were times when he wasn't even sure of his own health: battle waves conduce a kind of cumulative madness.

Every now and then there was a German soldier or two whose rehabilitation lasted for weeks and something resembling collegiality was possible. Marc recalled one boy from Metz who lost an arm. He spoke perfect English and was practicing learning to write with the only hand he had left. Then there was a middle-aged officer from Berlin who, ominously, refused to believe the war had ended and provoked an argument about it at every turn. Everyone chooses their own way to heal.

Marc approached the two amputees first.

Ich bin Dr. Greenspan. Sprichst du Englisch?

"*Nein,*" the first man replied.

"I do," said the other. "I can help."

"What is your name?" Marc asked.

"I'm Abraham. My friend's name is Friedrich."

"Hello, Abraham," Marc said. "I speak German. But if you don't mind, I can tell you what I know in English, and you can translate. It might be more efficient."

"Thank you."

Marc examined the men's wounds. Abraham had lost part of an arm; Friedrich one foot. Field bandaging could be slipshod, and men unlucky enough to be felled far from a decent hospital might die of infection before they ever had the chance to recover. It was something Marc had unfortunately seen scores of times. With the abatement and, finally, the conclusion of the battles, these kinds of surgeries succeeded far more often. That was the case here.

"You are both healing well," Marc said. "Tell your friend Friedrich if the crutches are working, the two of you might be able to go home by the end of the month."

"*Sie heilen gut,*" Abraham began, turning to speak to his friend. "*Wenn ich es die Stufen hinunter schaffe, kann ich es nach Hause Schaffen.*"

"*Ja, Ja,*" Friedrich said, smiling.

Marc laughed at the man's joke—'if I can make it down these steps, I can make it all the way home'. It was true: once you leave the hospital, everything else was as simple as rolling down a hill.

"Let me or Dr. Cordette know if you need anything," Marc added. He crossed the aisle and went to speak to the other new patient.

"*Ich bin Dr. Greenspan. Sprichst—*"

"—begging your pardon, doctor, but I speak English. I mentioned this to the other doctor when I was admitted, but he seems to have failed to inform you."

"I'm sorry." Marc consulted his notes; the man's name was Maximilian Berger. "Please forgive me, Herr Berger."

"Please call me Max."

"Okay... Max."

Max had been shot three times in his left leg; the first two bullets came out and were treated in a field hospital near Esternay in October, but the third one was near the knee and impossible to reach; it had to stay in. For a dangerously long period of time, Max faced the threat of amputation, but his condition stabilized. A treatment of Dakin's solution and a transfer to Paris for proper care followed, and now it seemed Max Berger was only a few days away from being released.

"You should be allowed to go home soon," Marc said.

"What if I don't wish to go home?" Max asked.

"I would think that would be a natural desire for everyone, including Germans."

"I'm not German," Max said. "I'm Alsatian."

"You enlisted in the German army."

"But Alsace is French now. Didn't you read about the terms of the treaty?"

"Actually, I haven't had the time to read the details," Marc said. "I've been too busy treating soldiers like you."

"I'm determined to stay in Paris," Max said.

"I don't really have anything to say about what you do or where you go after you are discharged from my care," Marc said. "But if your papers say you are a German citizen in the service of the Kaiser's army, I'm afraid sooner or later someone will spot you. You will be repatriated, whether you wish to be or not."

"You may call it 'repatriated'," Max said. "I call it 'exiled'."

"I'm sorry."

Over the course of their brief conversation, Marc took the opportunity to take the measure of the man. Max's English was nearly perfect, and Marc wondered how this proficiency was gained; he must have studied it in school. Max gave evidence of being educated and engaged, and this bode well for any future conversation for however long Max remained under Marc's care.

For a great while, Marc did not have much time to talk to any of his patients, but since the Armistice the opportunities had increased to the point where once or twice he actually had the chance to befriend one or two of them. There was a boy from Wichita who was an orphan; after his release, Marc met him for coffee one morning in December, and they promised to exchange letters once they both were home. After that, Marc sutured up a Frenchman from Lyon who invited him to come south and try his wife's sourdough loaves.

But Max was a different sort of specimen: a German fluent in English who disdained Germany. How did he end up fighting for the Kaiser? Physically, Max resembled the scores of landsmen who passed in and out of Marc's care across the years—hair the color of butterscotch, a slightly fat face, short and stocky but well-built. Yet there was something beyond these features that Marc could only classify as distinctive: a cheerful smile, a strong sense of independence, and an aura of action that made his current confinement seem twice as cruel.

"I'll come back to see you as soon as I am able," Marc said, patting Max's bed like he was about to tuck him in for sleep. "In the meantime, just keep resting."

"I've done nothing but rest since I've been here," Max replied. "But thanks, anyway. I look forward to seeing you again."

"That's the only direction to look these days," Marc said.

Some of Marc's colleagues refused to fraternize with the Germans, but he didn't feel that way. There were no sides to take once the war was over. "Where will you go?"

"There's a bunch of us living in Saint-Germain," Max said. "I'll stay there for now."

"Who's 'us'?"

"Alsatian refugees. One of them is my best friend. He found us a room in the shadow of the church. We grew up together and we served in the same unit. He managed to escape my fate, and after he was demobilized, he decided he liked life in Paris better than in Colmar."

"The two of you might be better off in Colmar," Marc said.

"Have you ever been to Colmar?" Max asked.

"No."

"Then don't consign me to that fate. It's horribly provincial. I get along well enough with my mother and my father, but if that's the best of it, I'd rather be here."

Marc recalled his previous opportunities for making new friends and decided to press his luck again here.

"If you end up staying in Paris, I wouldn't mind hearing from you. I'll be working here at least until the spring, so you'll know where to find me."

"That's very kind of you, doctor."

"You're most welcome."

Max sat up and whispered in Marc's ear.

"Don't tell the Prussian in the bed next to me, but I'm glad the Kaiser lost."

"Why is that?" Marc asked.

"Now my friend and I can march into the future and properly be citizens of the world."

"You don't strike me as a typical German," Marc said. Max smiled.

"And you don't strike me as a typical American."

Marc spent the rest of the day trying to puzzle out Max's meaning, but the pieces remained unresolved.

A week later, there was another letter from Sarah.

Jan 2, 1919

My dear Marcus,

I am concerned that I haven't heard from you. Christmas has passed, and now New Year's Day has come and gone, and still no news. When I hadn't received your replies in the past, I allowed all sorts of worries to overwhelm me — you were wounded, you were dead. Now with the peace I have nothing to go on but purely irrational fears. Did you get run over by bus? Have you caught the Spanish flu? I read daily of the plague sweeping across Europe and the rest of the world, and I long to know you are safe and well.

Enough of my complaints; other than my concern for you, I am well, as are mother and father. Billy Davenport came home last week; do you remember the Davenports? They lived next door to me when I was in grammar school, and Billy was nearly my first beaux. There was a huge party for him at the American Legion, and we all missed you. I am thinking about going back to school again in the spring. Without you to distract me (and a pleasant distraction it would be indeed) I have nothing to fill my days, and some sort of preparation for our lives together might be worth my while.

I will not resort to begging, and I forgive you if you are indeed overwhelmed with work. I miss you. Please write.

All my love, Sarah

A few days after receiving Sarah's latest letter, Marc wrote back.

16 Jan 1919

My darling,

I am so sorry not to have replied to your Christmas greeting, and I equally long for the day when we can be together again. Now that the Armistice has been signed, the soldiers are disappearing from Paris like grain flowing down a silo. I am still needed, of course—many dozens of men are still under the hospital's care—but the tide will recede, and I will come back to you as soon as I am able—with hope, by the end of the spring.

The whole of the city is bracing for the peace conference, which is to begin this week. It's like Derby Day everywhere you look – carriages full of dignitaries, motion picture cameras and photographers swarming the boulevards, and excited, purposeless crowds roaming the alleys and filling up the cafes. There is much deprivation if you have the eyes to see it, and we're all trying to steer clear of the flu. For the men in my care the hope for the future is measured, but all in all, I continue to believe that I am building a better world than the one I inherited.

I will try to update my reports as soon as I am able. Give my love to your mother and father.

Adieu, Marc

In his previous letters home, Marc had tried to explain his complicated feelings about the war—something of the terror but also of the passion—yet somehow the words never came out right. He tried to assuage Sarah's fears with confessions of his own, but his words rang hallow and each piece of correspondence seemed to increase and not decrease the distance between them.

While writing, Marc was prompted to remember a conversation he had with Sarah the week before he left for France. It was early April, and the willows along the park in Old Louisville were just about to burst with green. Marc and Sarah had arranged to share one last outing—a favorite pastime of theirs, a picnic. Sarah had loaded up her hamper with cheese sandwiches and bottles of root beer, and Marc plucked a sprig of dogwood from a tree and stuck it through a buttonhole in Sarah's cardigan.

The afternoon contained the possibility of being wonderfully idyllic, but then Sarah asked a question that Marc was wholly unprepared to answer.

"What will I do if you fall in love with someone you meet in France?"

"Why would you think such a thing?" Marc asked.

"I read all these stories…"

"Really, Sarah. I am hardly a Casanova."

"You don't need to be a Casanova to be attractive."

"Your fears are unfounded," Marc said. "I'm promised to you."

"Promises can be broken," Sarah said. "Or, over time, forgotten."

"Do you not have my engagement ring?"

"I do."

"Then you should cherish it."

"I shall, but the ring is no substitute for you."

"It will have to serve in my place, until I come home."

With that, Sarah burst into tears.

At the time, Marc had to wonder what glue would suffice to keep their union—soon so severely to be tested—intact. More than three years had passed since, and the substance of their love had been reduced to memories He was left with an impossible to express swelling in his heart.

Marc put his letter in the post on the day the Peace Conference opened, and then he forgot about it. It wasn't until a month later that he realized that the letters from Sarah had stopped coming.

II

Aurélie & Pierre

Aurélie Laprix was in want of a new hat.

This want wasn't due to the weather, although the winter had been colder and snowier than usual. It wasn't a sop towards fashion, either—due to the war or some other source of retrogression, last year's hats were still au courant. No, she found herself on the first floor of Au Bon Marché because that's where Gabrielle Sternberk wanted to meet her, and Madame Laprix could never pass through the millinery department without making a purchase.

Pierre, her husband, was not accompanying her today. This was not exceptional, as M. Laprix had better things to do than stand around all morning watching his wife choose a hat. He was an important figure in manufacturing and a deputy for the 8th arrondisement, where he and his wife lived in a townhouse inherited from François Beauchamps, Aurélie's father. In fact, Pierre's presence would have been unseemly, for he knew – as did all of chic Paris – that Aurélie and Gabrielle were lovers, and had been since the turn of the century.

In her youth, Aurélie Beauchamps was a great beauty; her green eyes and long chestnut-coloured hair were positively emblematic of the Belle Epoque in its glory days. She made her début at a ball in the Tuileries in 1898. She was seventeen years old, and already pursued by a score of suitors willing to wait years if necessary for the privilege of unlocking such a treasure. Not that Aurélie had any intention of waiting that long. She lost her virginity soon thereafter—first to a courtier's daughter in a suite at the Ritz, and then, more formally, to a young man named Henri who installed her in his apartment on the Champs-Elysées for an entire month, until Aurélie's boredom and Henri's habit of ignoring overdue bills drove them apart. François paid up and cautioned his daughter not to be so public in her affinities.

Aurélie might have continued in her pattern of seductions and displacements for eternity had it not been her misfortune to fall in love. Gabrielle Sternberk was at first merely another addition to young Mlle. Beauchamps' shiny string of pearls. She was in many ways Aurélie's opposite – a child of Slavic parents without a dowry, dark-eyed, moody, and nervous. But she also possessed something that Aurélie deeply coveted—passion—and Aurélie was used to getting what she wanted.

They met at a ball sponsored by the Société Jules Verne; Aurélie planted herself in front of a vase of gardenias and Gabrielle was ripe for culling. The two young women, barely out of their teens, began to conduct a torrid love affair.

There was, however, still the matter of extending her social standing, and that is why Pierre Laprix entered the picture. Although not known for his looks, Pierre received no shortage of proposals due to the importance of his position as a deputy and businessman. A decision for marriage was postponed until, like a bored chef in an under-attended kitchen, he discovered he had been stirring the pot too long and the freshness of the dish was gone. Then, like a glittering parfait, Aurélie Beauchamps appeared.

Monsieur Laprix was introduced to Aurélie at a party at the Belgian Embassy in the spring of 1906. Aurélie was now twenty-five years old, nearly too old to be respectably married, and all of society Paris was speculating on how she was going to extricate herself from this predicament. Pierre Laprix was heading towards fifty years of age and still a bachelor. One glance from the needy girl towards the reticent middle-aged man sufficed, and an arrangement was made.

They dined at Le Grand Véfour in the Palais Royale on the following Sunday, and by May they were engaged. Somewhere along the way, Aurélie slipped in her carnal knowledge of Gabrielle Sternberk and its subsequent importance to her well-being. Pierre was merely charmed, and their relationship had remained in perfect balance ever since.

Meanwhile, on the floor of Bon Marché, a different sort of balancing act was taking place.

"How about this one?" Gabrielle asked, lifting up a Reboux cloche.

"Too many colours," Aurélie replied. "It will clash."

"We could go to the atelier and choose one to order."

"Do you really want to make an especial effort just for a hat, Gaby?" Aurélie asked. "It seems disproportional."

"One can't always live one's life in perfect proportion, Aury."

"Speak for yourself."

And so the two women continued to bicker in front of the hat rack for a full fifteen minutes. The pair had smoothed down their congruent rough edges across the years well enough that nearly any sort of tangential disagreement turned into something resembling a scene from a play, filled with arch dialogue interrupted by quotable platitudes. The topic never really mattered; they could be discussing anything from the latest instalment of 'Jean-Christophe' to the quality of a steak. The goal was the performance.

"Let's look over here."

Gabrielle turned the corner and stopped in front of a table filled with berets.

"I'm not sixteen, Gaby."

"No, you're not," Gabrielle said. "But neither are you sixty. I've always held to the theory 'the older the woman, the bigger the hat'. Under my rules, smaller hats make you look younger."

"I don't wish to look younger," Aurélie said. "I wish to be younger."

"And I wish I was a Follies dancer. We're not here to wish, but to augment. Try this one." Gabrielle asked the clerk to hand her a black sailor's cap with a white leather band. She seized the cap out of the clerk's hand, nearly tearing off the label, and stood it uneasily on her friend's head. "No, I don't think so."

"Let me see," Aurélie said. "Is there a mirror?"

"Don't bother. It's far too dark. This one is better." Gabrielle lifted the clerk's bony hand and placed it upon a green tam-o'-shanter with a narrow scotch plaid ribbon. She caught the clerk sneering, but decided not to say anything. "Oh, yes. It will accentuate the colour of your eyes."

Aurélie sat in the chair as the clerk brought over a tiny table mirror.

"I like it," Aurélie said, shifting the cap from side to side as if she was posing in a studio. "I won't be able to wear it until the spring, but it'll be worth the wait."

"How about something else for winter?" Gabrielle asked. "I spot a shelf of woollen scarfs."

Their acquisitive barque sailed; thus was another half hour reasonably spent searching for a worthy port of landing.

Aurélie Laprix was not an undutiful wife. Although she and M. Laprix had no children, she was willing and able in every other way to play the role that she felt she had earned by marriage. She accompanied her husband to all the necessary engagements; it was an especially good excuse to freshen up the Worth gowns or air out the fox pieces. All the best charities knew to call on Madame Laprix when a boost was needed. Aurélie and Pierre entertained often, at least until the war put an end to conspicuous parties. The Beauchamps town house could easily accommodate twenty-five guests for dinner, with enough bedrooms for half a dozen to sleep over – or more, if the sleeping arrangements were kept strictly entre nous.

The couple had never been sexually compatible, and across the years, they had perfected ways of satisfying their curiosity without compromising their affinity. Aurélie, of course, had

Gabrielle; she considered her to be her true partner and, in fact, in many circles, especially those centred around Montmartre, the invitations would customarily read 'Mme Laprix and Miss Sternberk'. There were affairs with women on both Pierre's and Aurélie's part: in his salad days, the former once entertained a British actress who held only the minimal necessary knowledge of French while the latter recently improvised a weekend-long dalliance with one of Mistinguett's dressers.

Not all these affairs were conducted with women. Pierre flirted with men when he was young, but lacked the courage and the security necessary to act upon his impulses. Finally, when he was well past forty, he seduced a baronet from Limoges with the unlikely but exquisitely romantic name of Raphäel. Pierre and Raphäel spent a weekend in Bordeaux under the pretence of taking a tour of the local vineyards, but without any shared interests other than good wine and each other's bodies, they drifted apart. This was followed by sporadic encounters with suitable gentlemen, but Pierre never found any of them worth writing about in his private diary.

Pierre's urge for liaisons trickled out over the years, and as he approached the age of sixty, he was largely content to ogle young women in pastel-coloured dresses or young bow-tied men with freckles. His days were filled with factory plans and drafts of bills, and his nights were mostly spent sipping Courvoisier and smoking fine cigars.

Aurélie was loyal to Pierre, and dedicated to Gabrielle, but she had permission for (and was never averse to) seizing opportunities when they arose. Once, right around the time of the Battle of the Somme, Paris was overflowing with exceptionally beautiful and damaged young men who were particularly susceptible to the ministrations of an older, passionate woman. In particular, she remembered a soldier from Calais who couldn't have been more than twenty – and a virgin, evidentially – who kept calling her 'Emily' and spoke a French dialect that was nearly as incomprehensible to her as Esperanto. It seemed exquisite at the time; now she couldn't even recall his name.

The hour set aside for shopping was expended, and it was time for lunch. Aurélie carried the box with the hat and a bag filled with scarves and kerchiefs that Gabrielle thought might look good linked together like some kind of train. They dashed out onto the rue de Sèvres and made their way towards a café they liked that lay in the shadows of the church of Saint-Vincent-de-Paul. Their timing was poor, and they had to stand in the cold and the slush for ten minutes while waiting for a table. Aurélie wished they had gone to a place where she knew the maître d' and would have been spared any public indignity, but then she remembered that Gabrielle disliked fussiness.

When the food finally arrived, it was—as expected—quite good. Aurélie's impatience and disquiet melted away with the Camembert sandwiches and the strong tea.

"How is Pierre?" Gabrielle asked. She always asked.

"He has a bit of a cold," Aurélie replied. "And, of course, with a hypochondriac like Pierre, the first sign of a sniffle means the Spanish flu."

"I would hope not."

"Oh, I don't think so," Aurélie said. "Pierre has gone through at least a half-dozen influenza scares in the past three months. I'm liable to think if he hasn't caught it by now, he won't catch it at all. One can't hibernate all winter."

"His responsibilities must have increased."

"Peace is harder than war. In wartime, everything and everyone is focused on winning the battle—there are supplies, and communications, and charts and maps. All you have to do is connect the dots in the proper order, no questions asked. Then the war ends and, like someone turning on an electric light, there is nothing but brightness. The entire world is both obvious and yet impossibly brilliant. All the rules have been abandoned. But I'm not sure if I like exponential possibilities. It's quite unsettling."

"Are you going to that American thing?"

At first, Aurélie lost the trail of Gabrielle's re-routing of the conversation. Then she remembered: Pierre had received an invitation to an event – it was hard to tell if it was a ball, or a party, or a fundraiser, or all three – to be held at the Institut Pasteur, near Montparnasse, this coming Saturday evening. The current American ambassador, William Sharp, had been recalled, and his replacement, Hugh Wallace, was being introduced, and the staff of the American Hospital were being fêted for their service. Because of his patronage, Pierre had to be there, and – as his plus one for all formal occasions – so had she.

"Yes, I must."

"There's a lot of 'must' in the air these days," Gabrielle added. It was a heavy verdict, and it hung in the air over their table like an accusation. Aurélie felt the need to dissipate it.

"It might be amusing," she said. "Certainly, with the end of the war, at least the mood will not be oppressive."

"Will you know anyone there?" Gabrielle asked.

"I am certain of it. Pierre's on the board of a dozen advisory committees, and even before the war, he dragged me to all their luncheons. These people help at the Opera, or run one of the departments at the Louvre, or manage the gardens of the Tuileries, so I'm certain to find someone to talk with."

"I'd almost like to go, myself."

"Why? And be bored for two hours more than necessary?"

"I might find myself a new lover."

Aurélie laughed.

"Is your dance card that empty, Gaby?"

"Oh, it's not my card that needs filling."

The two women giggled like schoolgirls. It was nice to know after all the years and the war that it was still possible for them to shock each other. Once they had attained such a peak of amusement no further conversation was necessary.

"*La addition*," Aurélie shouted, raising two fingers in the air. They left.

Before the war, the Beauchamps' townhouse near La Madeleine was one of the district's most distinguished addresses. It was still so, but the new democratic urge made it déclassé to speak of it. There were fifteen rooms on three floors, with mahogany wainscotting and marble floors, all furnished exactly as they had been when Aurélie's grandfather built the house right after the Revolution of 1848.

Taste had changed, of course – Pierre switched out the dusky tapestries for some brighter Gérôme landscapes, and Aurélie replaced the busy china pattern with something glisteningly white – but the sense of settled purpose remained, and the house was a useful crutch to lean on as everything else in the world fundamentally disintegrated around it.

Still, every time Aurélie came home—be it from a shopping spree or from a liaison with Gabrielle or someone else, or even merely a walk around the block to clear her mind—she held on to an unmistakable sense that she was walking into a cage. This cage might be well-appointed and comfortable, but still there lingered the terrible feeling that the walls marked borders that should not be crossed. Because of this, Aurélie suffered from a constant need to escape.

Aurélie hadn't felt this way when she first married Pierre over a dozen years ago. In her way, she loved him, and he loved her, and furthermore he allowed her to continue to love Gabrielle Sternberk, believing it to be an entirely different emotion than the one he felt for her, something that certainly preceded him and was rooted in the comforts of childhood, as if his wife and her lover were playing with dolls instead of each other.

Over time, Pierre grew increasingly complacent and Aurélie, perversely, more unhappy. It was as if, with the realization that her husband was not fascinated by her split allegiance but merely tolerant of it, something of the challenge was broken, and the pieces were no longer worth the effort of being reassembled.

This led to the current détente: Pierre would continue to support Aurélie's sprees (although this was merely nominal, as the Beauchamps' holdings in property and bonds was worth more than all of M. Laprix's resources combined), and Aurélie would help to lift Pierre up to the level of respectability strictly necessary for a man of his position.

The fact that the two of them were play-acting the entire arrangement was neither surprising nor, in Paris, unique. The only rule the two of them agreed upon completely was that they would never create a situation where one of them might end up a third wheel; they conducted their lives along the patriotic lines of liberté, égalité, and fraternité, but of the three égalité was always paramount.

When Aurélie came home from shopping and lunch with Gabrielle, she was still hungry. The tiny cheese sandwich she ate at the café was delicious but decidedly unnourishing. Aurélie thought to ring for Marie to come up and bring her something, but as it was early afternoon and dinner loomed hours away she couldn't think of what that something could be, and she certainly wasn't going to leave it to the maid's taste or chance. She walked down to the ground floor, turned into the kitchen, and took a peek into the Kelvinator for herself.

The choices were slight. There were trays of unbaked pastries, a half-carved roast, lots of jars of sauces, a dozen eggs, milk and cream, and, incongruously, two baked potatoes. Aurélie thought the potatoes must have been left over from last night's dinner. She took a knife from the drawer and sliced off a well-done corner of the roast. The thing looked slightly imbalanced now, but Pierre would likely not notice and Marie wouldn't mind. Aurélie found a bread roll in the box next to the spices and improvised a sandwich. It would have to do until seven or thereabouts.

When she went back upstairs, she noticed the invitation to the Institut Pasteur event had been moved from the spot in the hall where she left it after opening it. The card now held pride of place on the table where the book recording all the important engagements was kept. That must mean Pierre had added it to his calendar.

"Darling, where are you?" she asked.

"Coming, Aurélie."

Suddenly, there was something to look forward to.

III

Aurélie & Marc

Marc thought if he ate even one more snail, he would be sick.

He had become inured to the contrasts between the lives of his colleagues—the physicians and surgeons, the administrators, and the staff—and the lives of poor Parisians, but he was still startled by the cornucopia laid before him. There might have been fifty guests in the reception hall of the Institut Pasteur, but there was enough food to feed twice that number. In a time of food shortages, even this small example of excess felt unseemly.

Marc spotted Paul Cordette standing next to the bar in the corner of the room nearest to the entranceway; he was holding a glass of pink wine in one hand and a red napkin with a piece of bread in the other. His familiar presence was like a lighthouse, and Marc navigated his way across the room in order to have someone to talk to.

"Moored to the hors d'oeuvres, my good doctor?" Marc asked. He plucked an olive with a toothpick in order to have something to do with his hands.

"More like submerged, I'd say," Paul replied. "I've been trying to get a word in with Dr. Roux all evening, but it's like asking for an audience with the Pope."

Having devoured the olive, Marc helped himself to the wine. Pre-filled glasses of champagne were lined up along the bar like a row of gilded trinkets at a bazaar.

"What do you need to talk to Roux about?" Marc asked. "Something you can't send up in a memorandum?"

"I'm sure the director has a clear understanding of our purpose as healers. I'm less certain of his knowledge of how the bureaucracy he has created here functions. We all speak competent French—at least, I do—and this division into language wards is inefficient. There are a hundred French soldiers for every ten Americans and siphoning off the German prisoners at this point is just plain silly. I came here to save lives, goddamn it, not to stand around fetching Dakin's solution and serving lemonade."

Marc laughed.

"My dear Paul, how many times have you played nurse? And what's the matter with you tonight? I don't think I've ever heard you curse before—at least, not since that time your needle snapped in the middle of an injection."

"Sorry, Marc. I'm just impatient, that's all."

"Have another slice of sausage while you wait."

"Ugh. I wish we could go someplace where we could find some real food. I can't make a meal out of canapés. Care for a late supper after?"

Paul Cordette had built up the continental habit of dining very late, and he had become especially solicitous of inviting his fellow doctors to join him. This was recent training for Marc's stomach; in America, he was used to dining around sunset. That habit was a remnant, he supposed, of his immigrant ancestor's days when food was limited to what was at hand and there were a half-dozen mouths to feed before bedtime and crops or animals to tend to at dawn. Marc found eating a meal close to midnight positively decadent.

"Let me hit this target first, and I'll let you know," Marc replied, waving a piece of bread in the air. Paul laughed and saluted.

"Carry on, soldier."

In addition to the introduction of the new ambassador, the evening was dedicated to a celebration of the now nearly completed work of the war staff of the American Hospital—with the subtle adjunction of raising money to reduce the overwhelming accumulated debt. Marc was neither a donor nor a solicitor; his primary function at the reception was decorative, but Paul, being one of the higher-ranking physicians, was required to mingle. He spun out onto the center of the floor.

A trio started to play a waltz, and there was dancing. Marc watched as Paul bowed graciously in front of a young woman in a short dress, and the two of them swirled out together. An evening which Marc thought of as a cocktail party was slowly evolving into something resembling an embassy ball. The social gears were gaining their grease, and an optimist might hope for some diplomatic spare change to float down from the effort in the form of bank cheques large enough to cover everyone's salaries.

Marc imagined how he would wish the remainder of the evening to go. If he was planning to dine with Paul, he could stop eating. He didn't mind dancing, but he was less forward than his colleague. Sarah knew Marc was far from a saint, but in public he wore the natural reticence of all fiancés like a sackcloth. Still, standing against the wall and nursing a drink was boring.

Marc spotted Paul and his dance partner out on the floor. The pair had been joined by another couple, an elderly man and a relatively younger woman. The woman was shimmying away; the old man merely pivoted. When the song ended, Paul came over with his newly assembled entourage. He introduced his dance partner first.

"Marcus, I'd like you to meet Adèle Forrestier. She's a charge nurse in the influenza ward. And this is Pierre Laprix and his wife, Aurélie."

"*Mon plaisir.*"

"Oh, we can speak English," Aurélie said. "It's such a more malleable language."

"Do you really think so?" Paul asked. "I was born in London, and I've felt hog-tied by British English all my life."

"I am pleased to meet you," Marc said. "What do you do, Monsieur Laprix?"

"I am a deputy in the Assembly," he replied. "But that's not really work, believe it or not. Before the war, I owned a manufacturing firm. Now I mostly coordinate suppliers and fill order books."

"Don't believe a word my husband says," Aurélie said. "Paris would absolutely cease to function without his efforts." Pierre smiled, and Aurélie took his hand. Marc noticed this gesture, and Aurélie noticed Marc, and for a brief second their glances crossed. Aurélie let go of her husband's hand and pressed Marc's into her own. "We all have a part to play."

"Dr. Greenspan and I are going to look for something more substantial to eat after this affair," Paul began. "Would you care to come with us, Miss Forrestier?"

"That would be lovely," she replied. "Thanks."

Paul turned to Pierre.

"Would you and your wife like to join us?" Paul asked.

"My wife would be charmed, I'm sure," Pierre said. "Unfortunately, I need to be at my desk in the Hôtel de Ville at eight in the morning."

"Are you sure, Monsieur Laprix?" Paul asked. "We'd be glad to accommodate your needs and make it an early night."

"*Mais non.* I'll be fine. My wife is used to representing me in my absence, and she makes for a much prettier landscape."

"She does, indeed," Paul said.

"You won't be far from my thoughts, Pierre." Marc thought he saw Aurélie smirk as she spoke this.

"I must say my farewells," Pierre said. "Good night, my dear."

Pierre kissed his wife on her cheek and disappeared into the throng bordering the banquet table.

"Where shall we go?" Adèle asked.

"I know a little bistro tucked in behind the Arc de Triomphe," Paul said. "There's usually not a crowd."

"We must go, *immédiatement*," Aurélie said. Her wish was interpreted as a command, and—once Paul and Marc had said their 'good nights' to their colleagues and helped the ladies fetch their coats—they were off.

In Louisville, Marcus Greenspan would have as much accepted an invitation to a midnight dinner with a pair of women he just met as jump into the Ohio River with all his clothes on. The approbation of the neighbors—who inevitably would be spying on his every move—let alone the long explanation necessarily to assuage his parents' curiosity would have entirely prevented such an event from occurring. But the years in France, especially on the front and in the midst of unprecedented carnage, had loosened Marc's need for propriety.

The four of them—Paul with Adèle, Marc with Aurélie—just fit into the back seat of a taxicab. Being pressed up against Aurélie gave Marc a golden opportunity to take a closer look. Madame Laprix seemed to be anywhere from thirty-five to forty years old; the brittleness to her talk and very faint lines around her mouth when she smiled sang of experience beyond that of an ingenue.

On the other hand, once pried away from her husband, Aurélie evinced the air of someone completely, even morally, free. Her dress, a brilliant shade of turquoise, hung tightly around her body as if it were a second skin and she might emerge from it, chrysalis-like, at any moment. Her hair was long, like a young woman's, and she wore it styled in a manner usually obtained only from the very best and most expensive salons.

Marc found it interesting—and just a little bit provocative—that Madame Laprix could be so easily unhooked from her husband and so blatantly enthusiastic about it. Monsieur Laprix was obviously much older than his wife, but that was not a novelty; perhaps she often exhausted him, and maybe he really did need to be in the assembly before breakfast.

All during the course of the ride, while Paul and Adèle chattered away about the snow, or the Peace Conference, or the unusual color of her leather handbag (it was lavender),

Marc and Aurélie sat together in silence. Aurélie was next to the window, and she appeared to be occupying herself with the view.

Marc wondered what Paul was up to. He knew, from their time working together, that Paul was a bachelor and unattached. He wasn't the type to brag of conquests, but beyond that there seemed to be the sense that there weren't any conquests to brag about. Marc had no idea if Paul ever had a steady girl. All that he had learned about his family was that he had a sister who was working as a nurse in Lille and his parents still lived in a village in Yorkshire in the house in which he grew up. The father was born in France, hence the family name and the inherited skill at languages.

Yet the bonhomie was there: this was not the first time Paul Cordette had seized the moment, taken the measure of the crowd, and stole off with his throng into the night. Even during the war, when there were blackouts and deprivation everywhere, Paul would never say no to a late-night buffet, or a couple of beers, or an improvised party. Marc wondered: *can two young men, free and unencumbered, be merely happy to be alive?* It felt like he was seeing himself in a mirror for the first time.

Marc had long gotten over feeling any guilt at spending time in the company of women other than his fiancé; after all, it was impossible for he and Sarah to be together as long there was a war. Marc had tried to straighten things out before he left for Europe, over an excessively long lunch in Louisville's Union Station just before he got on the train to New York. Sarah was grown up and independent, as was he, and out of respect for each other they promised never to lie or to deceive each other, but when the subject of fidelity came up, the details were left untended.

By the time the cab pulled up in front of an obscure café on the rue de La Pompe, Marcus Greenspan was ready for anything.

Marc was unexpectedly famished. His memories of the snails

and the toast points and the warm champagne at the Institut Pasteur had faded, and he relished the *plats du jour* the table had ordered, the warm bread the *garçon* had thrown into the basket, and the frothy pitcher of lager spilling over onto the small wooden table. Funny, Marc thought, before the war, French beer was worse than water. Now he was virtually a connoisseur. He supposed the Germans had made some positive contribution, after all.

Aurélie had positioned herself in the middle of her male escorts. She had just concluded a brief discussion with Paul about 'A Tale Of Two Cities'—one of the other times England and France and war were all jumbled together—when she turned her attention to her reference guide from across the ocean.

"What is life like in America?"

"I haven't been in America since 1916," Marc began. "So I can't really answer that question. But I can tell you something about life in America before the war."

"Before the war, before the war…" Aurélie said. "All anyone ever talks about is what things were like before the war, as if by talking about it, we can turn back the clock."

"You can learn about how things were," Marc said. "And that can teach you something about how things can be. It's called history."

"Don't be arch, young man," Aurélie said. "It's not becoming."

"He's becoming something, that's for sure," Adèle said. She had been resolutely silent up to this point.

"You're very amusing, Adèle," Paul said. "It's comforting to hear some merry words from you. And you are so young! Life must be very hard in the contagious disease ward."

"No harder than surgeon's work, or anyone else's," Adèle said. "And furthermore, I'm not that young."

"How old are you, then?" Paul asked. "We can go around the table and announce our ages."

"That's not becoming, either," Aurélie said. Then she laughed: "I'm thirty-eight."

"You won't get a peep out of me," Adèle added.
"I'm thirty," Paul said.
"You're a holdout," Aurélie said, turning to Marc.
"I'm twenty-eight," Marc began. "But I don't see why it matters."
"It doesn't," Paul said. "Nothing matters to me."
"How droll!"

Adèle giggled, and the waiter came by with a second pitcher of beer. Paul ordered another plate, demanding a larger portion of a particularly spicy saucisson for which all the others had sung praises while neglecting to leave a single slice for him. Marc noticed that Aurélie had, by very subtle traces, moved closer and closer to him, so that at this point her thigh was pressing into his and their arms touched each time they lifted their steins.

Marc thought this increased sensitivity to Aurélie's skin might be caused by his slight inebriation, but beyond that there was the lingering feeling that there was something deliberate going on. He knew French women were naturally flirtatious, but Aurélie was different. *Perhaps,* he thought, *I am imagining all this, and only thinking of it because I am lonely and missing Sarah.* Marc didn't usually think of other women as potential sexual conquests; they were friends and fun companions, unserious and unattached. Why had he chosen this moment to feel this attraction, to think these thoughts?

"What time is it?" Aurélie asked.

Paul reached into his pocket and pulled out a watch.

"Ten after one."

"The night is still young!" Adèle said.

"Not as young as you," Paul said. "But you still haven't told us how old you are."

"I thought you said it doesn't matter."

"It doesn't, but you have left the rest of us at a disadvantage."

"Guess."

"Sixteen," Aurélie said.

"Be serious."

"Fifty."

"Come on."

"Twenty-two," Marc shouted.

"You've hit the bullseye!" Adèle shouted, showing off her American slang. "You win!"

The four of them collapsed in a heap of laughter.

"I fear the night isn't quite as young as we had hoped," Paul said. "I really do have to get home."

"Where do you live?"

"In Batignolles."

"I'm in Clichy," Marc added.

"I have a flat in Saint-Germain," Adèle said.

"My husband and I live near La Madeleine," Aurélie said.

"We'll have to call four taxicabs."

"Nonsense," Aurélie said. "That's horribly inefficient and definitely anti-social. I'll find one, and he will take all of us home, one by one. I will pay for it."

"What if our driver is a woman?" Adèle asked. "Would you make the same demands?"

"*Bien sur*," Aurélie replied.

"But are you sure, Madame Laprix?" Marc asked.

"Oh, so now I'm Madame Laprix," she replied. "I revert to being your senior as soon as I take up the reins of responsibility."

"I didn't mean…"

"I am sure. In fact, let me pay for everything. *Mon plaisir*, as you so charmingly said when I first met you earlier this evening."

"You remembered?" Marc asked.

"I remember everything."

Even in as popular a neighborhood as Chaillot, it was hard to find a taxi in the early hours of the morning. Paul tried to be chivalrous and ranged the length of the block hoping one could be flagged down, but in the end, Aurélie produced a suitably capacious car simply by stepping into the road: beauty charms the mechanical beast. A blue Citroën pulled up, and the four of them crammed in.

Like a salesman making a pitch, Aurélie handed each of her fellow passengers her card as they drove across the city. Adèle disembarked first; her building was tucked in behind the Jardin du Luxembourg. She kissed everyone twice on the cheek and ran up the steps, audibly giggling like a schoolgirl. Paul was next; he lived on a narrow street facing the Parc Monceau. That left Marc and Aurélie alone for the ride from Batignolles to Clichy. Aurélie pressed her hands into Marc's.

"It was a wonder, meeting you as I did tonight," she said.

Marc did indeed wonder what it was that felt so special about their budding friendship. He paid particular attention to her phrase 'as I did,' as if she had experienced something extraordinary by the accidental crossing of their paths. The inside of the cab had grown warm during the ride; the closeness of Aurélie's hands and the touch of her gloved fingers made him feel flushed.

"I agree," Marc said. The comment felt stupid and unnecessary, but he could think of nothing else to say. The car pulled up in front of Marc's building. For the briefest of instants, Marc thought perhaps Aurélie was waiting for a kiss or something more, perhaps an invitation to come in.

"Good night," Aurélie said. "Please don't lose my card."

"Thank you for everything," Marc said. Aurélie laughed.

"I hardly gave you everything," she said. "That's God's work."

It was a curious comment, but again, Marc could think of nothing to improve upon it.

"Perhaps we could have lunch sometime," Marc said. "I'd like to get to know you better."

There, he said it.

"Call me anytime," Aurélie said.

Marc climbed out of the cab. The street was dark and cold. He watched the car pull away and disappear down the avenue du Clichy. He felt as if a page had been turned in what sages refer to as the book of life.

IV

Max & Django

From the time they were ten years old, Maximilian Berger and Django Bernhardt were best of friends. The two boys were neighbors in Colmar, a middle-sized commune in Alsace. Their parents lived in the same apartment building on the Harthgasse, one block away from the railroad station, and they attended the same insufficient elementary school, a cold and crumbling stone building in the center of town. No one was particularly interested in the education of two laborer's sons, and when they arrived at a common understanding of their poor situation it drew them together like vines.

Max was fascinated by his friend's qualities which, in nearly every manner imaginable, were the direct opposite of his own. Django was dark-haired and tall for his age, and Max was short, blond, and round; Django was adventurous and prone to troublemaking, while Max was literally a choirboy: he sang *Ein Feste Burg* every Sunday at St. Mathieu's. In their relations, Max was the pupil and Django was the teacher. Something about the smaller boy's neediness and the bigger boy's desire for demonstration made them a perfect match.

Django's exotic name was gypsy in origin, although there was never a jot of Romani blood in his family. When the boy considered it, he put it down as due to nothing more than his mother's strain of originality. He was an only child, and his unusual name singled him out. Most families living up and down the block shunned the Bernhardts—they were too diffident, too secretive—but Max was drawn to this son of a family of outsiders without at first ever understanding what his attraction meant; to him; it merely made Django special. Although both he and Max had German family names and lived in a German town, they knew something about their friendship was unmistakably if unidentifiably foreign.

Their bond was sealed one late spring afternoon in 1909 when the boys were twelve. A bunch of the older kids who lived up the hill in a nicer part of town thought to try to trick Django into surrendering the few measly marks he had in his pants pocket. When the surrender did not proceed as planned, it turned into an attack. Max and Django were outnumbered, but that did nothing to stop the former from throwing punches or the latter from ripping the shirt off one of his oppressor's backs. The battle was lost, but the two boys were forever linked by their joined fealty.

As the years passed, their bond strengthened, augmented by a pair of shattering revelations. The shattering of things is a rite of passage for all adolescents, but it was particularly keen in their case. First, as the boys' education advanced, so, too, did their knowledge of their tenuous social status. They were poor in a rapidly financially improving town, and they were German in a part of the world that once had been and, if a majority of the citizenry had their way, would once again be French.

The children in Max and Django's elementary school were mostly German speakers, the sons (and occasionally, daughters) of coal miners and factory workers, but when, at age fourteen, the boys began to attend a secondary school in the newer part of town, French was added to the curriculum. The boys boasted about their father's shops and the girls bragged about their mother's dresses. In the face of these class differences, Max grew shy, and Django turned resentful.

The second revelation was more profound than the first and cut deeper. When Max and Django turned sixteen and were supposed to be old enough to know better, they discovered they were more in love with each other than with any of the dainty burgher's daughters they met at the local candy store or were formally introduced to at dances or fairs.

Their love story began simply enough. One early evening, while walking together in the woods just outside the city walls, the two young men found themselves in that rarest and most freedom-inducing condition: alone. Django coaxed Max to sit in the shade of an ancient oak, and there he kissed him. It was the mildest of gestures, but it stood for some emotion that had long lain fallow between them, waiting to be cultivated. Django's kiss was the first act of affection from a friend that Max had ever understood, and it fit the description of the romances in the books he had read and thought he'd never experience for himself. He felt as if all of destiny had led him to that moment.

Unfortunately, teenaged boys have very little to say about destiny. Django and Max still lived under their parents' roofs. But sometimes opportunity can arise out of the most difficult of circumstances. Two months after their eighteenth birthdays (Django in May, Max in June) Germany declared war on France and England, and the friends became soldiers. Django did not feel particularly German, and Max, who was more robustly German, was instinctively drawn to anything that wasn't, but fighting was the only path open to them if they wished to escape. The week after war began, they enlisted and marched with their comrades towards the Somme.

The war scrambled Django's and Max's lives, as it did everybody's. They weren't patriots, but neither were they cowards. They held a strong sense of the need to defend themselves and the honor of Alsace, and although they much preferred if Germany had offered up the province voluntarily, they certainly weren't going to allow the French to just take it, like a plaything left unattended in the yard. The two men were still young and idealistic enough to believe that there was something worthwhile to soldiering, and their devotion to each other was easy enough to transfer to an abstraction like a nation.

Django and Max were mustered into the XVth Corps, comprised entirely of Alsatians and thus of dubious value to the Central Powers' cause from the start. They survived Verdun by being always in the wrong place, and they lived through the final year of trench warfare by developing a fanatical attraction to digging, as if by the simple act of imitating a groundhog their lifeblood would continue to flow.

Their maneuver worked. Several weeks before the Armistice most of the German troops in southeastern France threw down their arms and retreated across the Rhine. A smaller number—a number which included Maximilian Berger and Django Bernhardt—headed in the opposite direction. It was time to test the waters of the rushing river of peace; they decided to seek their fortune and their redemption in Paris.

It was a foolhardy mission, and only fools would attempt it, but Django and Max had each other for company and nowhere better to go. A life together back in Colmar with its bourgeois values and its prying neighbors was impossible, and now that they suspected all of Alsace was about to be returned to France their papers wouldn't be quite as damning as before.

There was always the risk of capture but being exposed as former soldiers of the Second Reich was likely less dangerous in Paris, where hordes had fled to escape their past. Their loving bond was equally less prohibited in a cosmopolitan setting such as the Left Bank. Django and Max thought of themselves, improbably, as a modern-day Hermann and Dorothea, adopting Goethe's heavily romantic sentiments as their own.

The two men slowly made their way across the French countryside, guided only by the shredded remains of their map. Despite the end of the fighting, their status as soldiers left them vulnerable. It took several days of hiding in barns and foraging for food before the real prospect of a future together could be considered.

Fate, however, had one more twist in store for them. Just

before Christmas, at the edge of a forest in Lorraine, two German snipers who had decided to ignore the truce spotted the pair of unidentified and possibly belligerent men and opened fire. Django found cover and was spared, but Max was hit three times in his leg.

His pain was earth-shattering, and the blood was profuse, but it was not a fatal blow. Django tore his undershirt into strips and bound the wound; he carried his friend a quarter of a mile into the nearest village. A dentist there with some knowledge of surgery removed two of the bullets and poured enough Dakin's solution over the third to keep Max alive until the wounds could be properly treated.

The weather was cold and Django was severely underdressed, but an insane determination to bring his friend to safety overrode all depredations. Fear of capture forced them to go by foot all the way from Saint-Mihail to Epernay, a distance of over one hundred kilometers; the journey took ten days. If not for the kindness of strangers who took no sides, the two of them would have starved before ever reaching help.

For a while, it was touch and go, and at one point Max drifted in and out of consciousness. In Epernay, they ran into a friendly and uninquisitive French medical transport team, and forty-eight hours later Maximilian Berger was in the American Hospital in Paris, one of the last and luckiest prisoners of war.

Django, now handed the role of sentinel, placed himself on guard for his lover's well-being and recovery. Their common enemy was now time, not men. Django rented a cheap room on the Rive Gauche while he waited for Max's release. There was nothing in the room but a sink and a bed; his only decoration was a 1918 calendar that he found for ten centimes on the boulevard Haussmann. The calendar was useless now that the year had passed, but the scenes of French scenery were colorful and comforting. Django hung it on a wall and opened it to January. The dates were wrong, but the numbers were the same. Django crossed off each one spent without his beloved like an offered prayer.

The doctors who ran the ward were exceptionally kind; they could finally afford to be. During the height of the battles, a man in Max's condition—injured but ambulant—might have been kept for observation overnight and then been forced out by overcrowding and left to heal, hopefully, on his own.

Now that the war was over, the crush was gone. There were free beds for the first time in years. By the end of Max's first week, the wounds from the two removed bullets had completely healed, and the one that remained in his leg had been cauterized and disinfected hopefully past the point of danger. He was only days away from being discharged.

In the meantime, Django came to visit every afternoon, arriving sometime after lunch and staying well past dinner. There were rules, of course—everyone had to wear a cloth mask to prevent the possible spread of influenza, and every visitor was supposed to be out of the building by seven. But the sight of the sobbing young man heaped at the foot of Max's bed for hours on end was too pitiful for Marc to oppose. Django's English was not quite as good as Max's, so it was up to Max to fill in the staff about their stories of shared childhoods and education, indifferent battles, and defiant luck. Max left out the part about love, but it was obvious to all, and especially to Marc. One night, Django stayed until nearly ten o'clock.

"Rest, my love," Django whispered. He was not particularly afraid of being overheard by the soldiers in the neighboring beds; no one in this current predicament was likely to make a fuss about a wounded man's affinities. But he needn't have worried : it was late, and everyone else was asleep.

"You should go home now, Django," Max said. "Go home and count the days."

Max extended his hand out from under the bedsheet and clasped Django's in his own.

"There are too many for me to count," Django said. Max smiled.

"You are still the same silly boy," he said.

"Is it so silly to want you home with me?"

"No, my love," Max replied. "It isn't silly at all."

The two young men sat together for a bit longer without speaking. Then Django stood up. He leaned over and kissed Max on the forehead.

"*Jus'qua domain*," Django said.

"That's good. Practice your French."

"*Au revoir.*"

Django's room was on the rue du Dragon, just around the corner from the boulevard Saint-Germain and the Brasserie Lipp. His choice of the neighborhood was not coincidental; after checking Max into the hospital and feeling reassured that the possibility of real danger had passed and learning that, despite orders, the authorities had no interest in shipping him back to Germany or anywhere else, Django headed over to the brasserie where he was told a solid community of expatriate Alsatians liked to drink.

The brasserie was one of the few places in the city where German was the principal language spoken, and its central location on the Left Bank meant not only workers but writers, painters, and socialists all congregated there. When he wasn't with Max in the hospital, Django liked to sit at a table at the back of the room and read the dog-eared copy of Novalis he found in a bookstore on the rue Bonaparte. There, he spent the few francs he had left nursing steins of beer or appeasing his palate with plates of oysters until closing time.

Django befriended the barkeep at the brasserie, an old man named Henri who had grown up in Strasbourg and was a young boy when Alsace switched from French to German fifty years ago. Henri took pity on the poor and hungry Django and offered him a free room above the bar and a job washing bottles for three francs a day.

The room was unheated, and the nights were freezing. The heat from the stove only radiated for about five meters and on snowy nights Django pulled the bed in front of the gas and huddled fully dressed under the one blanket. *Soon after Max is home,* Django thought, *I'll go out and get a better job, one that pays enough for us to find a warm place with a lamp for reading and some better clothes.* If Max could find work, that would bring in even more money and more hope.

The walls were bare, and Django couldn't afford to buy anything functional, let alone decorative; beside the calendar, his only extravagance was the purchase of a penny postcard he found in a junk shop on the rue du Four—a badly colored lithograph of the cathedral of Colmar. The church was Catholic, but the plain printed location was the point. Django felt that if he stared at the picture long enough, he could enter the tree-lined lane leading up to the church and see the pigeons roosting in the eaves.

But then, after another week had passed, something began to take the place of Django's need for Max. A yearning for what?—freedom, novelty, a different kind of future? His thoughts, which previously had been focused almost exclusively on Max and their future together, began to bleed into the walls and the building and, eventually, the neighborhood and the newness of the city. Despite his genuine love for Max, Django found himself fantasizing about other men, and then, in a displacement that surprised him as much as it drew him, discovering that the fantasy was not enough. He grew weary of sleeping alone.

Many nights he walked out onto the boulevards in search of company, and once or twice he found it. These incidents left a sharp and painful divide in his nature. Django was unwilling to completely give up on his devotion to Max; their impending reunion took on the shape of an old, familiar coat, one he was unwilling to think might possibly have lost its fit. Yet for centuries, willfulness has crumbled in the face of experience, and Django began experiencing all sorts of things that didn't include his friend.

Max was ready to go home on the 18th of January. The ward had arranged a little farewell party; the guests included Django and Drs Greenspan and Cordette, of course, plus four of the nurses who had helped with Max's care, a second surgeon who kept an eye on the infection, and five of the remaining soldiers—two Germans, two Americans, and one lamed recruit from French West Africa who couldn't understand any of the languages that were being spoken and merely smiled at everyone. The staff had pinned little paper pinwheels to the faded curtains and arranged cups of punch and finger sandwiches on a round table against the wall opposite the stairwell.

Every physician on the staff at the American Hospital covered shifts more or less equally, but somehow, over the course of Max's weeks there, Marc had become 'his' doctor, and so he was given pride of place to speak first.

"We all chipped in and got you a little gift," Marc said, handing Max a small box wrapped in blue paper.

"Thank you," Max said. He tore at the paper and opened the box. It was a little silver bracelet engraved with his first name in script.

"It's not every patient who is with us long enough to earn an engraving," Paul said. "We wanted to get you something practical, but we had no idea what you needed, so we chose this."

"It's quite practical to know my name," Max said. "Just in case I forget it."

Django stood at the foot of the bed and let the assembly shift in and out like well-wishers at a wedding. The nurses kissed Max, and the doctors shook his hand. From all that Django had heard from Max and seen for himself through the weeks of his confinement, there was an especial need to thank Marc Greenspan. While everyone who worked in the ward was attentive and all the doctors—physicians, surgeons, anesthetists, psychiatrists—gave Max the care he needed, it was Marc who singled Max out.

Marc had stayed next to Max's bed for a great part of that first night, when Max's fever was dangerously high and there was a constant threat of sepsis or shock. He brought him extra rations whenever possible, knowing that the natural ability of a young man to heal is augmented by healthy foods. Even after the fear had passed and Max had relaxed enough to sleep through the night, it was Marc who checked his chart more often than was necessary for the chance to sit with him to talk about the peace, or Alsace, or—and this was what Max found most curious—love.

One day, the topic of their conversation had flowed into the eddies of family life.

"I've a fiancé back in Kentucky," Marc said to Max. "Her name is Sarah, and we've known each other since we were kids."

"That's nice," Max said. "I've heard of Kentucky. Isn't that somewhere near the Mississippi River?"

"Not quite," Marc replied. "Louisville is on the Ohio River. But I suppose to a European, all of America looks like one huge blob."

"When are you going to be married?"

"We haven't set the date," Marc said. "But we've been engaged since before the war. At least, I think we're still engaged. I haven't seen her in more than two years."

"But you write?"

"Yes, she writes."

Max thought the construction curious, but before he could think of anything more to say, Marc added:

"I see your friend Django here every day."

Max wasn't sure what he could add to this statement that wouldn't sound insinuating, and despite the open atmosphere of the peace, he wasn't about to make his confession. Instead, he improvised something innocuous.

"We share a room on the Left Bank."

"That's an interesting part of the city," Marc said. "Artistic."

"I'm no artist."

"I didn't mean…"

"We like it there. Lots of Alsatians."

"Do you miss Colmar?"

"At times. I should write to my mother and father, to tell them I am alive."

"I can help you do that."

That conversation slipped away from the minefield that a further discussion of Max and Django's relations might have created, but a grain of something had been planted. Now, with the farewell party winding down, Marc felt a need to sow. He recollected Max's warm smile and his openness, so he threw caution to the wind and plunged ahead.

"I feel like we've struck up a friendship during your time here, and I am genuinely concerned about your welfare," Marc said. "If you end up staying in Paris for any length of time, I'd like to see you again."

"Thank you, doctor," Max said. "I think I'd like that, too."

"We've spent the entirety of our weeks together under the dull conditions of this hospital," Marc said. "Let's find a time and a place to meet that has nothing to do with my job. That way, we can talk more about something other than your health."

Again, Max noted Marc's careful construction of their time as 'together,' as if there was something out of the ordinary about his being a patient in this hospital. But he chose for now to ignore it.

"What should we do?"

"Here's my card. I've added my address and telephone number," Marc replied. "I live alone in Clichy. Let's have lunch someday soon."

During this conversation, Django stood next to Max like an attentive crow. Marc took a card out from his coat pocket and placed it next to Max's billfold and identity papers on the table next to the bed.. Max wondered if the fact that Marc lived alone was important and pertinent, and to this piece of wonderment, he added the thought that perhaps Marc's warm smile and genuine concern were evidence of something deeper. But all he said was:

"Thanks."

V

Gabrielle & Aurélie

It had been a long time since Aurélie Laprix could remember a disagreement with Gabrielle Sternberk, but here they were. The two women had just finished having tea at the Dôme in Montparnasse when the subject of Aurélie's recent flirtation with the Marquess de Fontaney came up.

"You're being promiscuous again, Aury," Gabrielle said. There was a single slice of a quiche Lorraine remaining on their plate and Aurélie felt it was a close race between reaching for her fork and making her reply. Gabrielle's remark, however, was hard to ignore, so Aurélie spoke and left the quiche alone.

"I don't know what to object to more," Aurélie said. "Your accusation of promiscuity or your implication of its repetition. It's as if my faith in you is of no value to you whatsoever."

As if to underline her refusal to give any quarter to Gabrielle's accusation, Aurélie proceeded to scoop up more than half of the slice of quiche and stuff it into her mouth.

"I still yearn for your faithfulness, darling," Gabrielle said. "It's something I cherish beyond cost."

"That's a laugh," Aurélie said. "Does your definition of faithfulness include that months' long dalliance with…what was her name?—the child bride."

"Eloise de Puyter? She was no child; she was on the cusp of eighteen. I merely served as her escort to a ball or two. That was months ago. I haven't the foggiest idea where she is now, nor do I truly care."

"With your own trail of conquests behind you, Gaby, it's no wonder you've lost track of them all. I still don't understand where your accusation of promiscuity comes from."

"You let down the Fontenay girl after a week," Gabrielle said. "At least I have the common courtesy of keeping my lovers close at hand long enough to learn their address."

"She bored me."

"Do you toss out all your girlfriends the minute the subject turns to knitting, or de Maupassant?"

"Really, Gaby. You're being petulant."

"All I ask for is a little stability."

"What? Is this your class consciousness percolating again? It's fine with you if I spend a month at a château in the Loire valley with some enchanted princess, but you draw the line for a night of unadulterated bliss with a concierge's daughter?"

"Now you're spinning fantasies. A concierge's daughter would be beneath you."

"Unless I'd prefer being beneath her."

"Very amusing."

Their argument, such as it was, had reached a kind of plateau. Aurélie was trying to decide between paying the bill and extending the conversation when Gabrielle made the decision for her.

"I'm tired. I want to go home."

Part of the problem of the terms of the relationship between Gabrielle and Aurélie was their divergent attitudes over the place they called 'home'. They'd kept separate residences all along, partially for dull propriety's sake, but also because they naturally feared their loving bond could be easily loosened by the daily boring repetitions that normal households naturally endure, such as checking the mail or sorting the laundry.

For Aurélie, home was the townhouse on La Madeleine and all the comforts that came with it, including, of course, a husband; for Gabrielle, it was an expansive but otherwise lonely flat facing the Place Vendôme with a lovely view of the Tuileries. Perhaps this difference in scale was one of the reasons that Aurélie took a lover more often than Gabrielle; after all, she had a longer list of items to rebel against, a fact which might, if taken the wrong way, have been what led to Gabrielle's accusation of promiscuity in the first place.

From Aurélie's point of view, any accusation of infidelity coming from her lover was a case of the pot calling the kettle black. Gabrielle Sternberk knew she was the type of dark lady that had proven to be like catnip to admirers both male and female since the dawn of time. She embodied the attributes of a raven—sleek, rapacious, swift, and flighty.

If she hadn't preferred the company of women, she might have gone down in the annals of literature as a great beauty but, alas, the men who wrote about such things never entertained her, and the ladies she seduced were too sated and too circumspect to publicize their liaisons. Still, anonymity only goes so far; the trail of broken hearts she left behind could be prominently found on any map of amatory Paris.

It takes a certain level of commitment to break a heart, however, and this was one of the factors that militated against any accusation of promiscuity on Gabrielle's part and freed her to toss the word at her partner's feet. Gabrielle conducted her affairs in the manner of a successful silver company, and with an equal amount of businesslike attention. Each lover was mined for as much value as could be extracted and then abandoned, sealed off and forgotten. The challenge, which Gabrielle was almost always willing to accept, was how to break another's heart without also breaking her own.

Her past was thus littered with small conquests. Before the war, there was a young woman from Shanghai named Jiang who stuck with Gabrielle for two months, just long enough to alarm Aurélie. Then, one morning in a suite in the Ritz, Gabrielle accused Jiang of stealing her Lippman wristwatch. The accusation was untrue, but it successfully ended the affair before the weight of it started to drag down more than just the interested parties or, even worse, involve the police.

Things got more interesting during the war, when there were more available women with increasingly desperate amatory inclinations. Gabrielle stuck to her own rule of never giving up on a romance while there was still a glimmer of a flame, but the lifespan of a glimmer was successfully narrowed down to a matter of weeks, and then—when even a week in Picardy could be trying—days. The only unchanged element in this new form of chemistry was the ownership of her heart. It never truly belonged to anyone but Aurélie Laprix.

Now it was February; the war and its depredations and subsequent changes to routine had been over for three months. The argument over the marquess was quickly forgotten, and things were starting to return to normal, if normal meant the freedom to come and go without fear of abandonment or jealousy.

All of Gabrielle's affairs were with women, which meant there was of necessity a comparative element involved; in fact, Gabrielle and Aurélie would often amuse themselves in bed by recounting and ranking their lovers as if they were racehorses at Auteuil. But Aurélie chose a slightly more dangerous path: she dabbled in men, and men—as time and history have proven over and over again—could always be counted upon to muck things up.

Aurélie's affairs with men were less frequent than her affairs with women, but because of this, they were more heavily fraught. For one thing, she was Madame Laprix, a married woman with a husband who had a reputation to maintain. This alone called for extreme caution, for one slight slip-up in the wrong direction—say, with a competing politician or an incorruptible official—could lead to a scandal. At times, Aurélie found it necessary to practically play the part of a detective, making inquiries of her prospective swains about professions, paramours, and finances. By being calibrated, this kind of love was always encumbered, figures on a chart with the passion merely colored in.

Once or twice in the past, the lure of romance threatened

her equilibrium. British officers were always game for a round of sport. In 1917, Aurélie met a young lieutenant from Manchester named Charles who had a taste for older women. She liked his mustaches and his muscles enough to ignore the difference in their ages and his annoying superior air. She told Pierre she was spending a long weekend in the countryside with a friend. Pierre suspected another lesbian fling and let it pass, and Aurélie Laprix and Charles Harding shared nearly the entire forty-eight hours of his leave in bed.

Later, after the weight of war grew heavier and the subsequent search for escape turned avaricious, there was a passionate week with an Irish pilot who was shot down and recuperating in a private ward near Saint-Denis, far enough away from Paris to prevent intrigue. In one of her rare acts of benevolence, Aurélie was volunteering in the unit assigned to the young man's ward, and everything spun out from there. His name was Laurence, and she almost thought of staying with him, until he began to grow needy and the whiskey ran out.

This triumvirate of lives—Aurélie's, Gabrielle's, Pierre's—had reached a point where it could almost be described as stable, with only occasional flare-ups of jealousy and the recalibrations necessary to assuage it. Their love lives compounded like any open market, with fluctuations and diversions whose regularity served as the best predictors of a profitable future.

But Paris in the winter of 1919 was anything but stable, and the new factors—the peace, the whirlwind of activity, the crush of visitors and foreigners, and, most of all, the wholesale realignment of everything from borders to social behavior—were rolled out like a gambler's dice on the green baize. It was anyone's guess which numbers would turn up and where the winners and losers would be found.

Two weeks after their meeting at the Institut, Marcus Greenspan called Aurélie Laprix on the telephone and asked if they might meet for lunch. He invited Aurélie to dine with him at a small café on the Île de Paris, right around the corner from the Pont Neuf and in the shadow of Sainte-Chapelle. He liked to choose meeting points with historical significance, with the wish that the timelessness of the place might rub off on any innocent witnesses.

Marc arrived first; he chose a table facing the window and was nursing an espresso when Aurélie came in.

"I grabbed two seats," Marc said, getting up to pull out Aurélie's chair.

"*Merci*," Aurélie said. She wore her good camel coat, and when she placed it on the back of the seat it trailed and touched the floor.

"Let me hang this up for you."

Marc picked up the coat and brought it over to the stand next to the bar. He turned to say something to the keep, and then came back to the table.

"I asked about the specials," Marc said.

"I never know what to order," Aurélie said. "And when you run into a creative chef, the dishes are things I never heard of."

"This man seems to lack creativity," he said. "I saw a raclette omelet and some onion soup, the ordinary *plats du jour*. Thank you for meeting me."

"You're welcome. I'm charmed. I may have lived in Paris for all of my life, but I don't have lunch with American doctors every day."

"What can an American doctor tell you that you don't already know?"

"For one thing, you could tell me about America," Aurélie replied. "What is life there like?"

But before Marc could answer Aurélie's very open-ended question, the garçon came over. He was about to recite the names of the specials but Marc beat him to it.

"I see you are offering an omelet, a *plat du saucissons*, and onion soup."

"*Oui.*"

"I'll have the onion soup," Aurélie said.

"The same for me." The waiter scowled as if part of the

fun of serving had been taken away by Marc's precipitate action. He put his pad in his apron pocket and walked away. Marc continued: "I always like to ask about the specials."

"Am I special, then?" Aurélie asked.

It was a forward question, but she knew Marc was prepared for it; after all, it was he who instigated this meeting.

"I would say that you are very special," Marc replied. "How is your husband?"

"He is very busy, but well, thank you."

"And how are you?"

This was a question which required more thought if it were to be answered truthfully. Aurélie was intrigued by Marc, even attracted to him, and by her reply she could either encourage or dissuade his pursuit, if that was what it was. It was early in the game, so she decided to stay neutral.

"I wish it were warmer, and I wish the boulevards were less crowded, but other than that, I would say that I am well."

"In my relatively brief time in France, Madame Laprix, I have learned that wishing is a lot less effective than doing."

"You must call me Aurélie."

"And you must call me Marc."

Their soups arrived. There was a natural pause in the conversation as they unfurled their napkins and arranged the silver.

"You haven't answered my question about America, Marc," Aurélie began.

"I had forgotten that you asked it. What did you want to know?"

"Tell me everything."

Marc went into a digression about Kentucky bourbon, and the Derby, and Harvard and studying medicine, and somewhere along the way he slid in a mention of Sarah Gold.

"We've been friends since forever," Marc began. "It all seemed so natural that we would be engaged."

"Engaged," Aurélie said. "We have the same word in French—*engagé*—but it sounds strange to me. It makes me think the two of you are like gears in a motorcar."

"It's a common term in English."
"Do you speak any other languages?"
"French and German. That was enough for this war."
"Do you expect another?"
"I guess that's what everyone in Paris is trying to figure out."

The waiter came to clear their plates, and they ordered dessert and coffee. So far, Aurélie had been playing by the rules. Marc was the one who asked for the meeting, so he had to be the one to advance things, or not. But one lull after another had stalled the conversation, and it had not taken on anything resembling a direction. It was time, Aurélie thought, to grab the bull, so to speak, by the horns. She brought their talk back around to the more dangerous subject of affinities.

"Tell me more about Sarah."
"What do you want to know?" Marc asked.
"The truth."
"Ah. Well, what I know of it, at least," Marc said. "She lives with her parents, in a brand-new bungalow in the center of town. She studied botany at university. She has a lovely smile. I get letters from her now and then just to make sure I'm alright."
"How old is Sarah, if I might ask?"
"The same as me, twenty-eight."
"You are young."
"The war has aged me."
"It does not appear to have done so."
"Thank you for the complement, Aurélie," Marc replied. "But it has aged me in experience."

"Ah, we play with words again," Aurélie said. "First, engaged, and now experience. Meaningless, without any context. What we are doing here right now is just as much an experience as the war."

"And what are we doing here, right now?" Marc asked.
"Nothing much…yet."

Aurélie leaned forward and pressed her hands into Marc's.

It was the exact same gesture she made when they first met at the Institut Pasteur, but then it happened in the presence of her husband and now they were alone.

"You are a married woman, Aurélie," Marc said. "And I am to be married."

"Would it shock you to learn I have taken a lover?"

"No, but after three years in Europe, I'm not easily shocked."

"Not only that, but it is a woman. I have known her, and loved her, since before I met my husband."

"What is her name?"

"Gabrielle."

Aurélie pronounced her lover's name with a deliberate sensuality, letting the breathlessness of the final syllable linger on her lips like a kiss. Marc felt it was extremely necessary at this point to take another sip of his coffee. It was the slightest of gestures, but it could stand for something resembling putting the brakes on the developing arc of their meeting.

Aurélie Laprix's behavior was seductive, and not only because of her openness and forwardness. She also exuded a brilliant combination of discretion and longing, of worldliness without effort. Marc thought, if only for an instant, of Sarah's girlish innocence, and her habit of accepting everything told to her or given to her at face value. Aurélie was neither innocent or guileless, and Marc felt himself being drawn to her like an acolyte to a priestess.

"Am I, then, to be another pearl in your string of lovers, Aurélie?" Marc asked.

"You tell me, Dr. Greenspan," Aurélie replied. "You tell me."

Once the barricade had been breached and the act of conquest instigated, Marc had no longer any need to prevaricate or delay. He thought about asking Aurélie to come back to his flat in Clichy, but then he remembered he hadn't taken out the trash, and since there was some beating of the rugs and shifting of the furniture that he had meant to do for a week, the whole of the place might strike a visitor who cared about such things as untidy. It was not truly suitable for a first impression.

There were many fine hotels surrounding the Île de Paris, but they were extraordinarily expensive. He was loath to consider cost in such a situation, but there was also the matter of habit: *Madame Laprix was certainly used to the best, and what would she think of me afterwards if I scrimped on our room?*

Marc also thought about Sarah, but this was not a new consideration. He had planned his response, both internal and external, many times before: they were engaged, but apart; they were adults, and subject to being lonely; the world was modern and forgiving. He thought less about Pierre Laprix—that was Aurélie's concern.

In the end, Marc put all his distracting thoughts aside and asked Aurélie if she wouldn't mind walking down the block to the Hotel Albe, across the Pont Saint-Michel.

She didn't mind.

Their room was indeed expensive, but that was not what Marc took away from his encounter with Aurélie there. He felt something exalted in the manner in which they approached lovemaking, as if it were not lust that was driving their consummation but art.

This sense of the beauty of it all began before either of them had removed a single garment; it hung from the walls of their room in the form of velvet tapestries and covered the bed in cream-colored silk. Even the silver cup holders on the bureau and the glass paperweight on top of the hotel stationery breathed of eloquence. The soft, reflected light felt holy, as if what they were about to do required a blessing.

When the time came to undress, after a first tentative and then a more assertively shared kiss, Aurélie kept to the theme of sanctification and placed each piece of her clothing on the edge of the bed like offerings. Marc remembered their discussion of age in the restaurant and marveled at the sleekness of Aurélie's body; it was the first time he had ever made love to a woman who was definitively older than he.

Marc followed Aurélie's lead. He put his coat and tie on top of her blouse and dress as if their garments were making the first moves and not their bodies, then he slowly stripped and climbed under the covers, issuing at last with his body the invitation he had only recently just formed in his mind.

For Marc, the hour they spent in the bed together was both familiar and new. He was modestly experienced in lovemaking (although never, to this extent, with Sarah) and knew how to serve as a patient and attentive partner. On the other hand, Marc was unused to Aurélie's assertiveness. She controlled every aspect of their encounter from position to process as if it were an improvisation, not unlike a mad accountant with a devilish proclivity for making and then fixing errors.

On her part, Aurélie relaxed once she was assured of command. The first thing she noticed about Marc's body was how muscular it was—a derivative of his youth, she supposed, but not surprising for someone as engaged as he had been in the tribulations of war. After that, there came bits of information—Marc's scent, the hairs on his chest, the strength of his hands—that functioned like ingredients in a recipe and turned the smorgasbord of their lovemaking into an orderly yet sensual feast.

When it was over, Aurélie dressed slowly, not because she wished to keep Marc around longer, but because she knew, as she had known many times before, that as soon as it was time to leave the room all of it would be converted to memory and shifted into a new world of recalibration, a place where it would expand into an aura or fade into a mist. Either way, things would change, and since childhood Aurélie had always been saddened by change.

It was nearly dark when they left the hotel. Marc vaguely recalled an appointment he had at the hospital at six o'clock and he wondered if he should take a taxi. They kissed in the middle of the Pont Neuf; the publicness of the gesture helped to seal their bond, to place it somewhere safe until it could be brought out again and considered in the bright light of day, like a treasure from a safe deposit box.

Marc put up his hand, and a taxi pulled over.

"*L'hôpital Américain*," he said. He turned to wave to Aurélie before he climbed in. Aurélie checked her bag and discovered she had left her hairbrush behind.

VI

Marc & Max

Near the end of February there was a tremendous snowstorm, followed by a hard frost. The denizens of Paris hid for a day or two and then, following their nature, burst out into a celebration of winter. Because the streets were unnavigable for any kind of creature bearing tires, automobiles lost their right of way to horse-drawn carriages. The muffs and furs came out of the closets, and the boulevards temporarily reverted to the serenely quiet places they were a half century ago.

Marc's response to this break in the routine was to take the afternoon off from work—it was not negligence; there were half a dozen empty beds—and go skating in the Bois du Boulogne. He had bought a pair of ice skates the previous winter but the weather hadn't cooperated at the time, and he only had one chance to try them out before the ice started to melt. The snow and the cold now beckoned; he threw the skates into the leather satchel they came in and headed to the park.

Marc was not alone in his quest for some precious time on the ice. When he arrived at the rink, there were dozens of skaters out there—mothers with daughters whose knees shook like fawns, semi-professionals making elegant figure eights, and couples holding hands and dancing silent waltzes. It was a matter of five minutes on a bench at the entranceway, and he was out among them. As for his skating skills, Marc was neither a dilettante nor a champion: he was fine on the straightaways and a little shaky making turns, but he avoided an accident and blended in with the crowd.

The poetry of the scene and the concentration required to stay upright brought Marc into a transformative mood. He was no longer in the Bois du Boulogne but inside an old Currier & Ives lithograph; he was not a doctor in Paris but an open-eyed teenager making lazy circles on Louisville's frozen Beargrass Creek and eager to make his debut at the ball called 'life'.

Marc was fourteen years old again, sitting on a wooden bench next to the frozen water and warming his hands with a mug of hot chocolate. His mother and father were in the picture, but not in his memory; his communion was with the ice-limned oaks and the charcoal-covered sky. *Why are the winters of my past so crystal-clear*, he thought, *and the present ones so enshrouded in cold mist?*

This sense of transportation lasted for a half hour or so. Marc skated off the rink and sat down on the bench to rest; he was thinking about taking off the skates and stopping to get a *café* from a concession stand when he spotted a young man smiling at him. The man looked to be around Marc's age, but under his blue woolen cap and with a thick white scarf wrapped around his neck there was not much to see beyond the smile. Good manners suggested Marc smile back, so he did, and the man came over and sat down beside him.

"*Bonne après-midi,*" he said. "*Je m'appelle François.*"

"*Parlez-vous anglaise?*" Marc asked.

"*Un peu,*" François replied. "A little."

"I'm Marc."

They shook mittened hands.

"I was about to go get some coffee," Marc said. "Would you like to join me?"

"I would be delighted."

The two young men carefully unlaced their skates; Marc stashed his skates in his bag and François tossed his pair over his shoulder like a sower with a sack of grain. They walked over to the stand. Marc ordered two espressos.

"On me," he said, as he handed the tiny cup to his new friend.

"*Merci*," François said. "I live in Auteuil."

It was an open invitation; the neighborhood was a mere ten-minute walk away, but since the topic of living arrangements hadn't previously come up, Marc wasn't sure what to say in reply. He suspected François was interested in more than just sharing skating experiences. He had befriended men like François in the past, friends in school whose touch was just a slight bit too familiar and soldiers on the front who were lonely and scared. He wondered how far he should meander into this fraught but fascinating territory.

Marc remembered one encounter in particular, years ago, when he was attending medical school in Boston. He was on his way home to his apartment on the Fenway and a boy—he couldn't have been more than eighteen—stopped him and asked for directions to downtown. Marc tried to help, until he realized the only direction this boy was truly interested in was one that led to a bed.

Marc was flattered and scared, but also intrigued. This was a situation he had thought about many times in the past, but he never had the courage to commit to it anywhere outside his imagination. Marc led the boy to a rooming house a block away from his apartment; he was allowed to entertain male visitors at home but he wasn't keen on raising suspicion. They took a room and went upstairs. In the end, they spent two hours in each other's arms. Marc hadn't done anything like that before or since, nor had thought about it again until now.

François sensed Marc's confusion.

"Wouldn't you like to come home with me?" he asked.

"I can't," Marc replied. "Not now."

"*Eh, bien*," François said. "It is always this way… 'I can't…not now…' What are you afraid of?"

"Myself," Marc replied. "I am afraid of myself."

"Maybe we can meet again someday," François said. "When you're not so frightened."

François got up, smiled again, and walked away. Marc thought, *frightened of what?*

The dénouement to this provocation occurred one week later on a freezing, rainy night. Marc was finishing up his rounds on the ward around eight o'clock when he heard a loud knock on the door. He went over to unlock it, and there was Max Berger. Max was sopping wet and shivering; he had no hat and the water was dripping down his face.

"Good God, Max!" Marc said. "Get in here. You will catch something awful standing out there in the rain."

"Thank you, Dr. Greenspan."

Marc brought Max into the office and settled him into the leather chair the staff used for interviews. He pulled down a blanket from the supply rack and threw it over Max's shoulders. Then he sat down behind the desk and asked the first question that came to mind: "What happened?"

"I know I should have called," Max said. "But the difficulty of finding a telephone and the hour…"

"Don't worry about that. We should find something warm for you to drink. But tell me, why did you come here?"

With that, the pathetic young man burst into tears. Marc jumped up and went to put his arm around Max, and that seemed to help. After a few seconds of coughing, Max was composed enough to continue:

"It was a silly argument with my friend," he said. "But, as the world has learned all too well, silly arguments can lead to lethal ones…"

"Lethal?" Marc asked, unable to hide the alarm in his voice. "Is someone hurt, or dead?"

"No, no. Only my heart."

"Let's not stay here," Marc said. "The night staff is settled. I'd check you in myself if I thought you required medical care, but that doesn't seem to be the problem here. What you really need is a warm room and a friend. I'll call a taxi and we'll go to my place."

"That sounds nice."

"I can put up a pot of tea and find you something dry to change into," Marc said. "And as soon as you're feeling better, you can tell me more about what is wrong. How's that sound?"

"I can't thank you enough, doctor."

"You should call me Marc. I'm not your doctor anymore.

"Yes, Marc," Max said. "I will go with you."

The ride to Clichy was brief and conducted in silence; the air between the two young men was heavy with tension. Marc thought of the questions he wanted to ask Max, but something about the necessary discretion and the distracted expression on the young man's face prevented him from speaking of them; Max was either too ashamed or too scared to say anything. They climbed up the stairs to the flat; Marc turned the key and they went in.

"I wasn't prepared for company," Marc said, surveying the usual unkempt condition of the room. "I'm sorry."

Max looked at the floor and grunted.

"Thank God you're a size smaller than me," Marc continued. "Everything I have will fit you with room to spare. Go into the bathroom and hang up all your wet clothes. Use the towel to get dry. I'll bring you some things."

Max puttered to the bathroom like a compliant child. Marc opened his dresser and pulled out some underwear, and then he went to the wardrobe and found a woolen shirt and a pair of flannel pants. He bundled them up and brought them in to Max, who was standing naked next to the bathtub.

In his nakedness, Max seemed especially vulnerable. Marc was reticent about comforting him with a touch, but beneath this reticence there was a definite urge to heal—the instinct of any doctor—and some form of physical contact was needed.

"You're still shivering," Marc said. He pulled two towels down from the rack; Max wrapped one around his waist while Marc used the other to dry Max's hair. It was as if Max was transformed into Marc's son and not his patient or friend, and

Marc was helping the boy get ready for his first day of school. Marc left the clothing on the counter.

"Put these on when you're dry."

Max unwrapped the towel and made a few more passes with it across his chest. He slid into the underwear and pants and pulled the shirt over his head. The pants were several inches too long, of course; Marc laughed as he cuffed the pants and the shirtsleeves, and Max took the cue and broke into a smile. They went back into the other room. Marc sat on the bed and motioned Max to sit next to him.

"Now, will you tell me what this is all about, please?"

Max started to cry again.

"It can't be anything worse than what you went through during the war," Marc added.

"I will start with a confession," Max said. "I owe you that much, at least. Django is not my friend. He's my lover. Oh, I know what you're thinking—'it's nothing but a stupid quarrel…a pair of pathetic homosexuals. Why did this crybaby come to me? Why didn't he go to some sissy bar and drink his silly problems away?'"

"I wasn't thinking anything of the sort, Max," Marc said. "And it's wrong of you to think I would."

"I'm sorry. It's just that when other people find out about me…"

"You wouldn't have come to me tonight if you thought I was the same as other people, Max," Marc said. "I hope you can trust me. Please tell me what happened."

"I was sick with jealousy, that's all. Django stayed out all night, and I confronted him when he came home, as I've done half a dozen times before. It's a routine I'd grown used to. After all, we made no vows to be faithful. I was about to forgive him—as I've also done before—when he told me he didn't think we should live together anymore."

"Why would he say something like that to you?"

"I don't know," Max replied. "I was surprised and shocked, and I didn't know what to do."

"Was it sudden?" Marc asked.

"For me, yes," Max began. "I asked him what was wrong, and I found out the truth. He told me he wanted to live alone; he wanted to be free. His vision of a life in Paris turned out to be completely different from my own. I imagined we would stay together in some kind of magical kingdom, like a pair of exiled princes, but for Django, I had turned into an accomplice, little more than a fellow escaped convict. I finally understood he didn't think we were fighting for each other, but for each other's freedom."

"How long have you been a couple?"

"In love? Six years. Friends? Forever."

"Then you must believe this is a temporary break."

"It didn't feel that way two hours ago," Max said. "To me, it felt like the end of the world. I walked out. Right now, I don't wish to go back."

"But why did you come to see me, of all people?" Marc asked. "I mean, I do understand why on a miserable night like this you didn't want to drink by yourself in a club or wander the streets. But surely you must have another friend in Paris, someone from the war who is close to you and who could take you in until you and Django reconcile."

"You were so kind to me when I was very ill," Max said.

"You deserved kindness."

"I felt you would understand."

"I do."

Max was about to speak, and then he changed his mind. He turned to Marc and put both hands on Marc's shoulders, and then he pulled him close to his body and kissed him on the lips. Marc was surprised, and confused, but the moment of confusion gave Max the chance to kiss him again.

"Max…" Marc couldn't think of anything else to say.

"You don't have to speak," Max said. "Just let me thank you. This is the best way I know how."

For Marc, gratefulness had never felt so fulfilling. In that instant, he thought back to all the time that had passed waiting for something like this to happen again, and all the time yet to come now rolling out in front of him like a red carpet. A door opened; Marc had to go in.

As they lay together in bed afterward, Marc tried to untangle his thoughts and retrace the steps that led him to that moment. He knew himself well enough by now to know that what had happened with Max was at least partially the result of his inability to resist a soul in need of love; it was perhaps the principal reason he wanted to be a doctor in the first place.

Marc grew up learning all the lessons of courtship and romance, and successfully suspected nothing wayward of himself in his dutiful following of the rules. He latched onto Sarah Gold as the subject of all his self-created myths, and as time passed the comfort he felt in these feelings protected him from temptation most of the time. But it had not protected him from the boy in Boston, or François, and it certainly could not protect him now.

The war, and Paris, changed things, but not, Marc thought, certain fundamentals: he was still magnetically attracted to need. The objects of his attraction merely expanded to include soldiers, with whom he assumed he must remain chaste, and other women, like Aurélie, where consummation was possible if disguised as another form of love.

Aurélie's charms were foreign and distant, a cornucopia of glittering surfaces. But what he did with Max was very different and upended most of his assumptions. Max was a man, like him—lost, like him—and as loving in return as Marc was giving, a mirror more than a vessel, with deep feelings that felt embodied rather than expressed. This was something unexpected and new.

Marc hadn't thought about all of this until the moment it happened, but when he did, he wasn't surprised by how he responded to Max's kiss. Marc grew up in a home without any brothers, but he had a lot of friends, and he knew how a keen combination of emotional turmoil and opportunity could lead to intimacy.

When he was training to be a doctor at Harvard, he read all about sexual deviancy, and he learned—through life-lessons more than in any of his medical texts—how truly un-deviant such attractions were. Marc suspected the only reason it had happened to him so infrequently was simply that very few of his acquaintances had the courage to ask. In his extreme need, Max was fearless.

"Tell me more about Django," Marc said. He had pulled on a pair of pajamas, and he hoped by retraining Max's thoughts on the partner he had left behind he might distract him for spending too much time thinking about the one that, minutes ago, lay beside him.

"I love him, for certain," Max began. "We've been comrades since we were boys together in Alsace. He was my best friend and my first love. As we grew up, it seemed natural to us to become inseparable."

"Perhaps that's one of the reasons why you find this current separation so hard to take," Marc said.

"After Django told me he felt we had drifted apart, I didn't know what to do. I told you we never swore to be faithful, but I hadn't thought about how I could go on living without him."

"That's a pretty cheeky thing to say after what you and I just did together," Marc said. "Our lovemaking felt to me like a pretty good way to go on living."

"What you and I did is so very different from what I have with Django. In the most obvious way, I'm only beginning to know you. It's exciting and fresh…unexplored terrain, so to speak. I was filled with gratitude for all you did for me and making love to you felt like a natural expression of it to me. But let's explore the past some more. I'd like to start at the same place you did. Tell me about your fiancé."

"Sarah? It's easier to be unfaithful when your partner is three thousand miles away, not four stops on the Métro."

"I don't know about that," Max said. "Infidelity is just as difficult whether the person you are cheating on is on the moon or in the next room."

"Now you're being philosophical, Max. One should never philosophize in the bedroom."

Max sat up. He was still naked, and he reached around and embraced Marc.

"What should one do in a bedroom, then?" he asked. "You must tell me."

"Ah, I thought perhaps sleep, although you seem to have rallied. Or are you hungry? It's too cold and stormy to go out. I have half a meat pie in my icebox, and there's a bottle of Sauterne in there, too. We could improvise a picnic."

"What time is it?"

"Almost eleven."

"Is it still raining?"

"I can't tell from here. Do you want me to get up?"

"No," Max replied. "Everything can wait. Right now, I want you to stay here."

Marc embraced Max. They kissed again and lay down side by side. If they had not been too distracted to hear to the sounds around them, they might have noticed that the rain had stopped and all the possibilities in the world were opening up before them.

The next day after work, Marc asked Paul if he wanted to have dinner somewhere in Battignoles. This was not an unusual request, and at first Paul thought nothing of it. But the point of the evening was raised almost as soon as the two young men had settled at a table in a small café facing the Moncey monument.

"I have a confession to make," Marc said. "And you are the only person in Paris I can think of to receive it."

"You know I'm not Jewish," Paul began. "It sounds to me like you're in need of a priest, not a colleague." He ordered a bottle of Crémant and some bread and cheese, to be followed by the Chateaubriand for two. "The food will help calm you down. What in all that is holy is the matter?"

"Maybe I'd better wait until after we've started drinking."

"Now you have me truly intrigued," Paul said. "Start at the beginning."

The garçon showed up with their wine.

"My head is spinning, Paul," Marc said. "I always knew of Paris' reputation as a dangerous place for romance. I'd managed to dodge Cupid's arrow up until now... but I've been seduced twice in the past two weeks."

Paul laughed so hard he almost choked on his drink.

"My friend, you surprise me to no end. Here I thought you were going to tell me you are joining the rabbinate, and now you reveal yourself to me as a tiger in disguise."

"I wouldn't go that far, but I do want to confide in you. Somehow, I feel you are a safe harbor."

"I am honored if a bit confused. Wouldn't this news be of more interest to your Kentucky bride?"

"Now you're being cynical."

"I'm an Englishman. I'm naturally cynical and bored by ordinary infidelity. If you don't add some salacious details to your story before our steaks arrive, I'll have to put you down as déclassé, and take out a book."

"First, there was Aurélie Laprix. You must remember her. We met at the benefit at the Institut Pasteur. She was there with her elderly husband, and you were escorting a young woman there—I've forgotten her name—and we all went off for supper together."

"I do remember," Paul said. "I was chaperoning Mademoiselle Adèle Forrestier. There was an older woman who left her husband in the dust. It seemed all quite innocent at the time."

"Well, that older woman was Aurélie Laprix. I called her a few days later and we met for lunch, and went to a hotel, and..."

"I get the picture."

"And then, last night, Max Berger came to the hospital sick and wet and desperate for my help."

"Maximilian Berger—the German prisoner with the infected bullet wound?"

"The very one. He's apparently a homosexual, and he had a row with his lover, and, well…"

"You mentioned two seductions," Paul said. "Dare I ask?"

"Oh, Paul," Marc said. "Max was so full of sorrow, and so much in need of love."

"I am pleased to hear you offered it to him," Paul said. "There's not enough of love in the world today. I just hadn't imagined you were available in that manner. You must have assumed a new position in order to accommodate Max, and please don't take that literally."

"I'm afraid between the two of them, I assumed a lot of positions that were previously unknown to me. Aurélie is ten years older than me, and Max is six years younger…"

"Max is also certainly a man," Paul said. "And an extremely handsome one, at that. Did you not think I noticed?"

"What do you mean?"

Just then, their steaks arrived. The conversation stopped as Marc passed the salt and Paul poured from the second bottle of wine. Then Paul almost immediately picked up the slack.

"Have you never wondered about my own proclivities?"

"I know you to be a gentleman," Marc said. "I know you to enjoy the company of women."

"Women make fabulous company, it's true, but—if I may be as frank with you as you were with me—I prefer male bedfellows. I hadn't made a point of telling you this because I never felt the need. But boy, do I feel it now."

"I should have sensed it," Mark said. "Is that why I feel so comfortable talking to you?"

"You are blessed with a sixth sense," Paul said. "And instinctive luck. You might have fallen into a bit of trouble confessing to Dr. Roux."

"What should I do, Paul?"

"I'm glad that you are comfortable enough about all this to take me into your confidence and ask for my advice, but it's far too early in your story for me to tell you what to do. In fact, I believe that it's far, far too early for you to try and tell anything of the sort to yourself. Why would you wish to extricate yourself from such an interesting and provocative ménage? Let it all in, Marc—the world and all its wonders. Don't you think, after everything, you deserve it?"

"It's true, Aurélie Laprix is a fascinating companion," Marc said. "My hours at the hospital and my evenings alone or along the boulevards lacked sophistication, and she is a font of it. She's made it clear she lives a life independent from her husband, whom she evidently still loves, and at this early juncture I see no reason to deprive her of my company, or for me to deprive myself of hers."

"So far, so good…"

"And Max is young and passionate—qualities that suffered grievously throughout the war. I suspect Max will eventually, if not permanently, gravitate back to his beloved friend, but without a vow of chastity or a forced faithfulness I see no reason not to encourage him to test the boundaries of his love."

"If this all wasn't so fantastically true, I'd say it was unbelievable. After so many years of restrictions, it's delightful to discover love can be a two-way street—and a crowded one, at that."

"Isn't that so?"

"I'm happy that you came to me," Paul said. "It puts me in the position of being your sage advisor. I much prefer that role—a sidekick is easily kicked aside—and I am older than you, after all. But now I must ask: are you familiar with the places you could go in Paris with Max where you could act openly together?"

"No, but I suspect you are."

"I am, although most of the time I am unluckily alone. Let me know the next time you and Max have plans, and I'll take you on a Cook's Tour of Gay Paree."

The discussion had been so engrossing that Marc had almost forgotten there was a meal in front of him, but somehow, over the course of the conversation, the plates had indeed been cleaned.

"I enjoyed my evening with Aurélie as well," Marc said.

"You could alternate your lovers, like flipping a mattress—turn things over when one side wears out."

"You're being cynical again, Paul."

"It's my natural philosophy," Paul said. The wine glasses were empty. Paul tilted his as in an invitation for more, but Marc deferred. "This has been a most enlightening evening, Dr. Greenspan."

"I'm glad you found it so. It's been mostly perilous for me."

"Perilous? How so?"

"I'm not used to wearing my love on my sleeve, and I'm certainly confused," Marc said.

"If love is not confusing, it's not doing its job."

"I didn't know love is a job."

"Heavy labor, with no time off. Now, I think I'd like some coffee." Paul lifted his finger and summoned the garçon. "*Due cafés, s'il vous plait.*"

"Thank you, Paul. You don't know how grateful I am to have had this chance to speak with you about all this."

"You are most welcome, Marc," he said. "Just be glad you didn't put yourself into the middle of even more of a complication."

"How so?"

"You'll be pleased to know you're not my type."

VII

Marc & Paul

By the beginning of April, actions on the world stage were heating up, with the heart of the fire emanating from the Peace Conference in Paris. Woodrow Wilson had proposed his Twelve Points and crossed the Atlantic Ocean twice; the heart of the Ottoman Empire was reincarnated as Turkey; Czechoslovakia was carved out of Austria-Hungary, and Alsace and a piece of the Ruhr were taken from Germany and given to France.

Away from Versailles, the little earthquakes of life continued as well. Marcus Greenspan had slept with Aurélie Laprix three times, and with Maximilian Berger twice. Despite the global consequences of the actions of the various diplomatic corps, it was these latter facts which had preoccupied Marc for the past weeks. When the entire world is a banquet, it is simpler to focus on what's on the end of your fork.

Let it not be construed from this that Marc was uninterested in the tides of human affairs or unconcerned about the welfare of his fellow man. Not once over the course of this time did he neglect his duties at the hospital or ignore the headlines in the Paris Herald—(except, perhaps, for the time when he and Aurélie spent the night barhopping in Montmartre and didn't get to bed until five in the morning).

But men (and women) are naturally self-absorbed, and Marc's principal goal in that peaceful and complicated spring was to sort through his feelings about love, and specifically the love of three people—his fiancé in America, his married paramour, and his male partner. It was, on the surface at least, a complex mess.

Against all odds, it turned out to be Aurélie who offered the simplest path to resolution. Unlike Max, she had a home and a husband, two traditionally steadying factors in any relationship, and unlike Sarah, she was at hand. Aurélie also had another lover to distract her when Marc was otherwise occupied with work or with Max.

Despite Aurélie's genuine affection, Marc felt his nights with her were, without making too much of a fuss about it, more or less another entry in her daybook, right alongside—and possibly no more or less important than—having lunch with an old lover or ordering a new evening gown. Aurélie's steadfast and uninflected attention to everything was very reassuring and helped Marc to counter his sense of being inside a maelstrom. She was passionate about her affair with Marc, but then she was passionate about Gabrielle, and chocolate, and Coco Chanel, too.

Because Sarah was out of sight it was simple, too, to keep her out of mind. Marc rehearsed in his mind how he might go about explaining what was happening to him when the chance arose to do so, but the idea seemed so distant and abstract that he never felt compelled to give it anything more than the amorphous shape of a dream.

Max was a harder nut for Marc to crack. Max couldn't (or wouldn't) go back to the flat he shared with Django, so for the first week or so after that rainy night in March Max temporarily took up residence in Marc's small and untidy flat. Marc borrowed Max's key and made a series of surreptitious runs back and forth from the boulevard Saint-Germain to the flat in Clichy to rescue some of Max's clothes and books and trinkets, each time wondering if he ran into Django would he have to fight a duel or settle matters over steins of *doppelbock*?

The establishment of the new household solved one problem but created another: Marc's bed was nowhere near big enough for two men to sleep in comfortably. The bed would have proven to be equally small for a man and a woman, but no woman had ever tried to sleep in it. Beyond that, there was barely room in the flat for the furniture, let alone another person's belongings.

Marc's eminently practical solution was to find a bedsit for his friend, a single room (with a single bed) on the rue Baudin, across the street from a cemetery and a mere four blocks from Marc's place—a stopgap measure until Django was either restored and his prince returned, or a larger place could be found. This, of necessity, limited the amount of time Marc and Max could spend together, but also increased the intensity of that time and helped to polish their relationship until it resembled a shiny jewel.

It was this shininess that Marc was contemplating that morning in April. The weather was beautiful; it was one of those rare early spring days when the breeze is both cool and warm at the same time. The tiny, unfurling blossoms were ripe with promise, and he felt, once again, as if anything he imagined was possible.

Marc was waiting to meet Max at a café on the boulevard de Chapeau; it was an anonymous sort of place that just happened to be more or less centrally located, equidistant from Marc's flat in Clichy, Max's room, and the hospital. Marc had an hour before he needed to be at work, and he had several important points of order to discuss with Max.

Max arrived, looking for all the world like God's gift to man. He was wearing the buttercup-colored Oxford shirt and the crimson linen jacket that Marc had bought for him on a whim, and which Max knew pleased his lover immensely. Max's hair had grown in, and it flopped across his brow and over his ears and made him look younger than twenty-two, and subsequently—in Marc's eyes, at least—more appealing.

It had proven difficult, over the weeks, for Marc to get past these visual manifestations of his newfound happiness; it was one of the reasons he thought of Max as 'shining' and also the principal motivator behind his need for this meeting: this blinding light had to be adjusted, or it was just possible Marc would never have a clear view of things again.

Marc thought of Max as the missing piece of a puzzle which he had been spending nearly the whole of his life to solve. Although he had been aware of his attraction to men, and even acted upon it in the past, it was never part of his picture of the future—a green but hazy place with a wife and a house and, perhaps, children. Before Max, desirable men were present, but impossible; Sarah fit the bill but was temporarily out of the picture. When Max came along, the puzzle suddenly made more sense; the completed composition was of Marc's love of one specific man.

"*Bonjour*," Max said, pulling out the chair opposite. They kissed, French-style, cheek to cheek.

"Hi, Max. Coffee?"

"Yes, please."

It had been nearly a week since they slept together; it might be a week until they could do so again, and so the flush of recollection and anticipation flowed through their conversation.

"I wanted to have the chance to talk with you about the future," Marc said. There was no need to dither. "Our future."

"I've been thinking about that, too," Max said.

Marc wondered if he might allow his friend free passage to speak first, which would make his job easier but also possibly less his own. He plunged ahead.

"That's good. I'd rather not leave all that we feel for each other unspoken."

The girl arrived with their coffees.

"I've never known you to leave much of anything unspoken, Marc," Max said.

"That's true. But here it is—in order for us to live together, I'd need to find a bigger place. A bigger place means a more expensive place, and a more expensive place means we'd need to find a way to bring in more money."

"There are a lot of conditional statements buried in that speech," Max said. "The most important of them being 'for us to live together'. Have we yet spoken about whether or not this is something we want to do?"

"It would simplify some things."

"....and complicate others. You would want to continue to see Aurélie?"

"Yes, I suppose."

"You suppose? I would hope you would have a more definitive opinion on the subject."

"I haven't spoken to her about it," Marc said. "I enjoy her company, of course, but continuing on in my current manner with the both of you would be...how did you put it?—complicated. I wanted to talk to you first."

"I am flattered, but you have told me in the past that you didn't wish to give either one of us priority, something about fairness."

"Well, I have to broach the idea to one of you before the other," Marc said. "I could hardly call for a conclave and schedule a vote."

"That would be most modern of you, but you must remember I haven't even met Madame Laprix yet."

"And I hardly know Django," Marc said. "We haven't yet touched upon how you feel about him. He must have changed since those days when he came to visit you in the hospital, but have you?"

"Do you think Django is the same to me as Aurélie is to you?" Max asked. "For one thing, I am not currently sleeping with Django. He is no longer my lover."

"But he once was that, and more," Marc replied. "How am I to know what the future holds?"

"And not a word about your bride-to-be in America," Max said. "Have you completely forgotten about Sarah Gold?"

"Of course not. I still plan to go to America, and to see Sarah. What I don't know is when that will be, or what I will say to her when I get there."

"It seems to me that the simplifications you so earnestly hoped for and spoke of a moment ago are slipping further and further out of your reach."

Marc fiddled with his now empty coffee cup and checked his pocket-watch. It was ten to nine; he'd have to be at the hospital in forty minutes. Suddenly that forty minutes felt like hours.

"It's not a competition, Marc," Max continued. "A month of us has taught me not to make demands you can't meet, or ask you for things you aren't willing, or ready, to give me. So hearing you talk about moving in together frightens me. I love you, of course, and I'd be willing to find a job to help pay my way, but I truly don't wish to hurt your relations with Aurélie or Sarah or force you to choose."

"Why don't you allow your practical American friend a little rationality?" Marc asked. "Frankly, I thought about asking you to do this because the whole of it would save us both money and time. I wasn't going to stop seeing Aurélie, but obviously I can't live with her the way I can live with you."

"I'm still not sure how I feel about having to share you with another," Max said. "It really is of no consequence to me whether it's a man or a woman."

"Truly?"

"Well, no. I suppose I'd be more jealous of another man. But it's pointless trying to be rational about affairs of the heart, don't you think? Love affairs that depend upon rationality are doomed to respectability."

"No, my dear Max," Marc said, taking his friend's hand. "Love affairs that depend upon rationality are houses with strong foundations. Let me help to build us that house."

Marc met Aurélie three days later; they took their usual suite in the Hotel Albe and spent the time making love. For Marc, this was unusual and strangely engrossing; whereas his forward motion with Max was characterized by its shininess—a feature of the daylight—all his time in the suite with Aurélie had an edge of savagery, abandon, and night. There had to be rules somewhere, but at that moment rules felt like the last thing on his mind.

There was a moment, after the two of them had finished and they lay spent on the enormous bed, when Marc actually managed to balance in his mind images of the two kinds of lovemaking he was experiencing—with Aurélie and with Max—that was so concise and clear that they might as well have been illustrations in a manual, if such a thing could be so equivocal regarding one's choice of sex in a partner.

In bed, Aurélie behaved like a big cat; she lolled and purred and spread her arms out, grabbing hold of the bolsters like she was in heat. Her long hair flowed down over her breasts and across her back, and she teased Marc and held him with a spider's sense of possession. Marc responded to Aurélie's teasing and testing like a boy enjoying punishment, a thrilling combination of guilt and transgression.

And yet, with his eyes closed, Marc couldn't also help but think of Max, especially Max in the situation he now found himself with Aurélie. The feeling was less of a comparison and more like a choice of dishes at a restaurant, completely different but equally satisfying.

Max was not only younger and smaller than Marc, but his needs (as compared to Aurélie) were also milder. He liked to let Marc stay on top, and he was patient to the point of often forgetting what they were doing while they were in the middle of doing it. Max's approach to lovemaking was similar to the way a ten-year-old boy thinks about fishing—it really didn't matter if anything was caught; the pure act of spending time in the company of his friend made him entirely happy.

"How is Max?" Aurélie asked. Marc was startled, wondering, for a moment, if Aurélie was able to read his mind. Aurélie lit a cigarette, a recently acquired habit that she claimed she was unable to pursue at home with Pierre, who had a perhaps not entirely irrational fear of house fires.

"He's well," Marc answered. "I was thinking of asking him

if he wanted to find a flat with me."

This was a little lie, as Marc had already done the asking, but it was a defensive maneuver necessary in case it raised a furor.

"Should I be jealous?"

"My darling, I thought you already were," Marc said. "But no, I wouldn't ever think of leaving you. It's just that Max is so lonely living alone, and he and I would save money if we shared a place. You have Pierre and Gabrielle, and I have you, and…well, this way, Max could feel like he has someone, too."

"That's terribly mercenary of you," Aurélie said. "I might add that you'd have the chance to fuck him more often, too."

Marc laughed.

"Don't be vulgar, Aurélie. It really doesn't suit you."

Aurélie snubbed out her cigarette and reached across the bed to put on some clothes.

"Are you hungry yet, my dear?" she asked.

"Only for you," Marc said. He rolled over and kissed her on the spot between her breasts. Aurélie pushed his head down and held it there.

"I can satisfy some of your needs," she said. "But a good croque monsieur is beyond my capability. Let's get dressed and go downstairs. Michel is in the kitchen tonight."

They left the mess for the housekeeper to clean up.

When Marc was alone, he continued with the maddening and likely unresolvable task of comparing Aurélie's lovemaking to Max's. It was a fresh topic; one he had never considered. That the two of them were biologically different was a given, but, as Marc had learned all too well, appeals to the heart are not exclusive to either men or women. Marc had already formulated Aurélie as the maestro and Max as the tyro, but that was a simple conclusion reached by comparing their ages and years of experience; the gist of the difference was something much less apparent.

It took a number of experiments and far too much self-consideration before Marc finally understood what it was in his nature that could be satisfied at different times by both of them. Aurélie was a teacher and an explorer; she had long passed the point where any man could surprise her with technique or dazzle her with jewels or furs. She approached making love to Marc with the keen eye and dedicated patience of a watchmaker, applying a tender touch to his belly or the briefest of kisses on his lips like a match to straw.

After sleeping with Max, Marc concluded that Max had never had sexual relations with anyone other than Django, and his was a limited experience, at that. Max talked often of how much he had loved Django, but when Marc tried something new with him in bed, Max reacted like he had never heard of it before. Many times during their lovemaking, Marc would suggest something higher up on the intimacy chart than mere kissing or fondling, and Max would ask, pleased but bewildered, 'can you do that?' The result, in the end, was like a taffy pull in Marc's mind: he was expanding his experience with Aurélie and then applying it as if it were a course of study with Max.

If it were as simple as admitting to himself that he preferred men to women, or even Max to Aurélie, Marc would have not felt so distracted. But the thing that one expects to happen in any situation where a comparison has to be made hadn't happened yet. In the presence of such unfettered joy, Marc found he had forfeited his ability to choose.

A slight tick in one direction was advanced on the night Marc and Paul went to Pick's.

Samuel Picque's club had been one of the favorite meeting places for homosexuals of all stripes since before the war. Let the drag queens fill up the tables at LaRue or the tuxedoed lesbians linger along the bar at Le Monocle; Pick's was an ecumenical temple of lust. There you could find willowy blond boys and female truck drivers, linen-suited businessmen and ball-gowned ladies (and men). A band played dance music on the ground floor; upstairs there was a piano bar, and the basement was a partitioned dungeon where couples or trios or orgies could be conducted with various levels of privacy.

Pick looked like a pervert and cultivated this look by keeping his hair long and wearing a worn-out military coat complete with epaulettes. He was over sixty; his wrinkly face was always beaming a yellow-toothed smile. His anti-chic appearance of course made him most fashionable and his club the ultimate 'in' spot. On any night of the week—especially between the hours of midnight and five—men and women and everyone in-between would line up along the boulevard Montmartre waiting to get in.

Tonight, Marc and Paul had to wait twenty minutes.

"I'm so glad I've finally had the chance to show you Pick's," Paul said as the maître d' brought them to a table next to the stage. "One can't really appreciate the place until you get close to the dawn, and you keep such a beastly schedule."

"I don't know how you do it, Paul," Marc said. "You're two years older than me, and you have just as much responsibility at the hospital as I, if not more. Yet you burn the midnight oil like you had access to a pump."

"My dear, you have your German soldier and your French lady to keep you occupied. I need to hit the marketplace every now and then."

"Are you as craven as all that?" Marc asked.

"Oh, I didn't mean that literally. I'm still young and handsome, and I can find someone to keep me company without any fuss if I wish. But it's the gayness and the joy of the place that I feed upon. During the worst of it, this was practically the only place in Paris where I truly felt at ease."

"And now, the worst of it is over."

At Pick's, the composition of the staff was as variegated as the clientele. You might equally be served by a teenaged boy in a sheer bathing suit or by a middle-aged gangster's moll in a black beret and fishnet stockings. The crowd was always mixing things up: the fat businessmen would chase after the half-dressed boys and the overdressed young men who clerked at Printemps by day threw extravagant tips at the molls.

The band struck up a ragtime version of 'After You've Gone' and the tiny floor filled up with dancers, a quarter of them men dancing with men, another quarter women dancing with women, and the balance a mixture of couples of indeterminate sex.

"Would you care to dance with me, Marc?" Paul asked.

"I'm not really a very good dancer."

"And I'm not a very good partner. We'll make a perfect pair. Come on."

Paul led Marc by the hand, and the two young men gravitated to the center of the floor. Over the course of the spring, Marc had grown fond of Paul and envied his freedom, but this was the first time the two of them had gone out for a night on the town together. It was one of the rare evenings where Aurélie and Max had other plans, and Marc didn't feel a particular need to catch up on his sleep.

Marc wondered, as Paul put his arm around his waist, if Paul was secretly hoping for a liaison. The likelihood of such a thing had grown more possible as the two of them shared their secrets. After Marc confessed his affairs and his confusion about them, Paul spoke of his longings and his loneliness. Marc knew how easily kindness could transform into lust; after all, it had happened with Max. But he believed his friendship with Paul was too valuable to ruin over sex.

The song ended, and the two men returned to their table. Someone had left a single red rose there. Paul picked it up, and one of the waiters signaled to them from behind the bar.

"*Le homme à ta gauche*," he shouted.

Paul turned around to see a tall, very skinny middle-aged man with a fedora smiling at him and waving him over to his table.

"*Mais, non*," Paul said. He knew the man could not hear him, so he shook his head violently in order to underline his reply. The man feigned a look of disappointment and smiled.

"Does this happen to you often?" Marc asked.

"Every time," Paul replied. "I've found I have to be quite choosy if I want to find someone. It seems as if everyone who wants me is old and decrepit."

"We'll be old and decrepit too, one day," Marc said. "It's always best to be kind."

"Kindness can get you into all sorts of trouble, especially here," Paul said. "Did you enjoy our dance?"

"Yes, it was fun. Maybe I should take lessons."

"That's a wonderful idea. I could ask around."

"Do you mean for the two of us?" Marc asked.

"Why not?"

"I suppose. Don't you get enough of me at work?"

"I never get enough of you," Paul replied. "You know that, and you know I'm not fishing for a compliment, or a chocolate on my pillow, for that matter. You're my best friend."

"Yes, Paul," Marc said. "You're my best friend, too."

"Then we must make this a regular outing. I'm having a blast."

"I can't stay up this late very often," Marc said.

"I promise, I'll get you home before you turn into a pumpkin."

"It's the carriage that turns into a pumpkin, not the passenger."

"Let's get another drink."

"*Eh, bien*," Marc said. "There's no stopping you, is there?"

"I'll stop when I'm dead."

Paul called over their server. He was one of the new ones, a young man in a leather harness and vest.

"Hello, handsome," Paul began. "What would you recommend for two very thirsty boys?"

"*Du lait*," the boy said, and then, after a beat, he added "*Avec* Courvoisier."

"Just bring the brandy, my boy, two measures," Paul said. "We can get mother's milk at home."

The boy rolled his eyes and ran off. Paul was just about to ask Marc if he wanted to dance again while they waited—likely for longer than they'd hoped—for their leather-clad server to return with their drinks when four policemen with loud whistles came running down the central staircase.

"Oh, *merde*," Paul shouted. "It's a raid."

"What should we do?"

"It's too late to make a run for it," Paul said.

The policemen split into pairs and started herding everyone towards the exits.

"Looks like it's time to go."

"Are we going to be arrested?"

"Arrested? In this town?" Paul replied. "The police have no interest in arresting anyone. If anything, they are merely plying the crowd for good-looking boys to pick up on the sly. They'll collect their usual bribe from Pick or one of his minions, and then they'll close the place for forty-eight hours so it looks good on their monthly report."

"I guess you're used to being herded by gendarmes," Marc said.

"Nobody's herding me. I am making a dignified retreat. Don't forget your coat."

Paul and Marc followed the crowd up the stairs. One of the policemen—an older man with a grey handlebar mustache—amused himself by prodding one of the more effeminate men with his nightstick as he passed by. Marc couldn't help but notice one of the other policemen—a young one, with very tight trousers—was locking arms with a man with a footballer's build.

"*Quel excitation*," Paul said as they took in the shock of the cold air on the boulevard Montmartre.

"It's enough for me," Marc said.

"Oh my dear, get ready for a lifetime of it," Paul added. "If this is what you want, dig in. It's all a moveable feast."

VIII

Pick

One of the reasons of going to a popular nightspot is that you never know who you might run into. Sometimes the encounter might be thrilling—a celebrity, an old friend, a new lover—and at other times, it might be disastrous: a sworn enemy, a political adversary, or a former partner. As everyone knew, Pick's was the kind of place where all of these possibilities could occur, often simultaneously. Showing up was a roll of the dice, and most of the patrons were incorrigible gamblers.

The negative possibilities never dissuaded Gabrielle Sternberk from planning an evening there. She had known Samuel Picque for years, since she was a teenager. The two of them represented two types of people who are always attracted to each other; she was an exotic beauty with an empty dance card, and he was an entrepreneurial queen looking for way to attract customers.

Pick's approach was as simple as planting Miss Sternberk at a center table dressed in a pearl-encrusted sheath dress, and then telling the band to play something quiet and romantic. One by one, every man in the room (and perhaps half the ladies) approached her and asked for a dance.

From the beginning, Gabrielle knew that saying 'no' was a successful strategy for an unending future of yeses. After Aurélie entered the picture, Gabrielle naturally tempered her behavior, but she never quite abandoned her role as a scandal-seeking adventuress.

She recalled one memorable night last October, when peace was in the air but there was still the slim possibility of German interference. Aurélie had a pressing engagement with Pierre, so Gabrielle staked out their usual shared center table on her own. The years dropped away; by eleven, it seemed as if every eligible bachelor or debutante in Paris was swarming her environs. The band switched from ballads to rumbas, and at one point Gabrielle led a conga line of bare-chested men around the palm trees as if they were all in Polynesia.

After the conga dancers had been dismissed and dispatched, Gabrielle turned her attention to a woman sitting by herself at a banquette near the staircase. The woman was nursing a vodka gimlet and smoking a cigarette in a foot-long holder. She offered Gabrielle a light; Gabrielle offered in return a few hours of unspeakable pleasure, and the two of them retreated to the basement. It was well past dawn before they were spotted again, entwined in a lounge chair at the foot of the piano bar and sharing a hookah.

When Gabrielle and Aurélie went to Pick's together, the evening would take on the flavor of a private party; nearly all the other patrons in the room would be their friends or acquaintances, and those who weren't—the teenaged boys, the overweight shipping agents, or the plain daughters of middle-class businessmen—would pair up and quietly leave or move up or downstairs where they wouldn't compete with the main event. Aurélie would make request after request of the band, and they'd shut down the place at dawn.

Marc and Max were always slightly more circumspect in their behavior when they went to Pick's. There were two reasons for this. First, they had naturally reticent personalities when compared to Gabrielle's and Aurélie's; women are always able to get away with the sort of things that were likely to get any man hauled before a magistrate. The other reason was that both of them, for separate reasons, were less than confident about avoiding someone they didn't wish to see. It was a generally foolish fear, but foolish fears can be just as visceral as serious ones and just as often can turn out to be true.

Their second visit to Pick's—the one after the raid—turned out to be innocuous. The regular house band had taken the night off to play for a ball in Fontainebleau, and Pick had hired a Spanish guitar player whose soft tangos and gentle merengues induced calm and actually allowed for conversation. The two young men sat together in the back of the room drinking warm beer; they danced a little and left around three to return to Clichy for a few hours of peaceful lovemaking.

Such happiness could easily lead to complacency; it was with just such a lowered guard that Marc and Max returned to Pick's near the end of April.

The evening went well at first: the two of them arrived around eleven, and they were hungry. They ordered pickles and cheese (Pick's signature dish, chosen for the pun on his name) and a bottle of champagne, and they spent their first hour watching the mating game take shape. The band came on, and they danced. Everything seemed to be heading towards a satisfactory conclusion. But then Aurélie and Gabrielle arrived. Gabrielle was apparently already drunk, for as the two women were brought to their usual central table, she tripped over a chair leg.

"What should I do?" Marc asked Max. He spoke in a stage whisper because the band was in the middle of blaring out something resembling a march.

"Is this my chance to meet Madame Laprix?"

"I suppose I always knew that the two of you would meet someday," Marc said. "But I had hoped it might be over an innocent luncheon, and preferably without Miss Sternberk."

"Do you and Gabrielle Sternberk not get along?"

"I met her once, for ten seconds. I was having dinner with Aurélie at Maxim's, and she burst in and handed over a string of pearls."

"That sounds like the beginning of a short story."

"It was a very short story."

The young men's debate, such as it was, was brief, for after Gabrielle regained her composure and the two women were seated, Aurélie did her customary scan of the room and spotted Marc immediately. She abandoned Gabrielle and rushed over to Marc's table.

"*Mon cherie!*" she said, leaning over and kissing Marc on his forehead and then on each cheek.

"Hello, Aurélie.

"And you must be the legendary Max."

Max had stood as Aurélie approached, and now he took her hand and kissed it.

"I'm no legend," Max replied. "Just an ordinary man. It is a pleasure to meet you at last, Madame Laprix."

Aurélie let out a horse laugh.

"What's with this 'madame' nonsense? Surely we must begin on a first-name basis. After all, we share a lover."

Marc was used to mild indiscretion, and he expected as much from Aurélie, but he was nevertheless startled by her openness.

"Aurélie…"

Marc stood up with Max when he saw Aurélie approach, but now he was sitting again, and trying, unsuccessfully, to deflect things.

"Do you and Gabrielle have plans to meet anyone tonight?" he asked.

"If we did, I would abandon them."

"Would you like to join us?"

"Gabrielle and I have already placed our orders," Aurélie said, as if the arrival of a Pimm's Cup was enough to glue her to a specific spot in the room. "But certainly we should all sit together, *n'est pas*? Anything else would be pointless."

"And awkward," Marc added.

"Are my boys shy?" Aurélie asked. "I would think we were beyond that by now."

Marc grew wary when he heard himself and Max referred to as 'my boys,' but there was no way he could think of to extricate himself from the situation other than leave, a rude gesture which would certainly lead to unpleasantness and perhaps a future act of retribution on Aurélie's part. There was nothing to do but acquiesce. He nodded to Max at the same time that he pulled up two chairs so as to not leave his friends stranded on the edge of his decision.

"We can all squeeze in here," he said.

A minute later, the four of them had more or less formed a huddle. The table was obviously too small, and their drinks were in constant danger of tipping over, but the closeness of it helped smother Marc's discomfort. Aurélie, of course, felt nothing of the sort.

"I've lived and loved in Paris for almost twenty years," she began. "But this is a first—just look at us!"

"I hadn't thought of the symmetry of it until now," Gabrielle said. "Two men, two women. You'd think we were normal."

"If we could only get Max into bed with Gabrielle, we could close the circle," Aurélie said. Max's response was to stare intently into his cocktail glass.

"There's only one problem with that supposition," Marc said. "Max doesn't sleep with women."

"And Gabrielle doesn't sleep with men," Aurélie added. "So we're even."

"I wish you'd all stop talking about me as if I wasn't here," Max said, finally.

Marc turned to Max and gave him a very gentle kiss on his cheek.

"It's okay, Max. Aurélie won't bite."

"Tease me enough, and I just might," Gabrielle said. Max looked alarmed. "I'm kidding."

"I'm afraid I'm not as sophisticated as the rest of you," Max said.

"How old are you, Max?" Gabrielle asked.

"Twenty-two."

"Well, no wonder," she said. "I would be aghast at any young man who showed signs of sophistication at your age. Now is the time for you to be innocent and exploited."

"And how would you wish to exploit me, Miss Sternberk?"

"Oh, I wouldn't be the one to do it," she replied. "We've already established you're immune to ladies' charms."

"I protect Max from exploitation," Marc said.

"That's one kind of love, I suppose," Aurélie said.

"What do you mean?" Max asked.

"Nothing at all."

"Tell me, Max," Aurélie said. "Do you prefer we speak English, or French, or German? Gabrielle and I are fluent in all three. She speaks Czech, to boot, but that's neither here nor there."

"I speak the universal language," Max replied. "The language of the bottle. Let's order another."

"I'll drink to that."

Gabrielle Sternberk was apparently not drunk, just clumsy. She ordered a second bottle of champagne for the table. When the band started in on 'I'm Always Chasing Rainbows' they all got up and danced. Marc partnered with Aurélie, and Max partnered with Gabrielle; the latter pair looked ridiculous, as Miss Sternberk was half a foot taller and insisted on leading. Then they switched partners and relaxed; the song ended and they returned to their seats.

Marc had just finished refilling their glasses when he looked up and saw Paul Cordette come into the room with, of all people, Django Bernhardt. Max followed Marc's gaze and muttered '*Schiesse!*'

"What's the matter?" Gabrielle asked.

"It's my colleague, Paul Cordette," Marc began. "And he's with Max's old lover."

Paul spotted Marc. Playing the faux naïf, he came directly over. Django lingered beside him. Paul put out his hand.

"Good evening, Madame Laprix," Paul began. "I can't believe in all this time that we've never bumped elbows here before. I hope you remember me. I'm Paul Cordette, Marc's colleague at the hospital. And this is Django Bernhardt."

Django smiled and bowed. There was a precipitous moment

where the six of them stood as still as statues, as if without Pygmalion's intervention they might never resolve into motion again. Then Marc broke the uncomfortable silence:

"Hello, Paul," he said. "Join us?"

"Hi, Maxie," Django said. He was still standing, although by this point Marc had stood up and pulled over two more chairs.

"Please join us," Marc repeated.

"Django and I are childhood friends," Max said, hoping this slight evasion of the truth might smooth over the rough edges of his predicament. "We served in the war together."

"I've heard you two were more than friends," Aurélie said. "But it needn't be awkward. We're all grown-ups here."

"Do you want to go, Max?" Marc asked.

"No, please, everyone," Max began, three words pointing in three different directions. "Aurélie is correct. There's no need for drama. Let's be kind to each other. It's two o'clock in the morning, and we've all lived through enough unpleasantness in the world already."

"I suppose if we sit here long enough, every one of our ex-lovers might materialize to haunt us," Marc said. He thought perhaps a joke might help to lighten the mood, but Aurélie only heard the word 'haunt'.

"I would hardly like to encounter a ghost," she said. "There are plenty of them in the world, too."

"How have you been, Maxie?" Django asked.

"I think about you often," Max replied, not answering the question, or perhaps answering it obliquely. The only people who had ever called him 'Maxie' were Django and his mother.

"I'm sorry," Django said.

"You have nothing to be sorry about, Django. You needn't apologize to me."

"I would like to do so anyway."

"I accept," Max said. "I am well and happy, and I hope you are, too."

Gabrielle raised her empty glass.

"I think this marvelous confluence of love requires another round of toasts," she said. "How about a bottle of Lafite—1893 was a good year, I hear."

By the end of the evening, which was, in fact, dawn of the following morning, all the parties involved felt they had more or less settled their scores and come to a relatively polite accommodation, speeded up by several bottles of exceedingly good champagne.

Paul had the easiest task; he had befriended Django only a few days ago, when they ended up on the same bench in the Jardin des Plantes. Paul recognized Django from his visits to the hospital, of course, but there they had been very formal with each other.

Alone in the garden, they struck up a conversation and went for a drink, and after that—once the joint attraction was apparent and the horizon of opportunity came into view—Paul brought Django back to his place in Batignolles. They spent the night together making love and trying very hard—most of the time successfully—to avoid talking about Marc or Max. They had become inseparable ever since.

Aurélie and Gabrielle were merely amused by the confluence of lovers, especially on Gabrielle's part. Her serial coupling across the years had often put her in the position of running across past partners in every imaginable place from the restrooms in Maxim's to the carousel of the Louvre. And Aurélie mostly felt dispossessed, having to stand aside and watch Marc's current swain parry with someone from his past.

Although she would have loved to have been a fly on the wall to the ensuing conversation, Aurélie silently agreed with Gabrielle that in this instance, discretion would be the better part of valor. The two of them excused themselves, claiming an imaginary engagement for breakfast in Le Marais.

When it was just Paul and Django, and Marc and Max, the four of them were able to pretend the party had resolved into something resembling a double date. Max and Django behaved politely to each other, and the conversation turned to how well Max's wound had healed and who Django had taken in as a roommate (it turned out to be a young man named Giorgio from Milan who washed dishes by day and sung ballads at a café on the Boulevard Haussmann at night).

Max, on his part, was consumed by a bitter longing for his friend; it was as if all their years together belonged to a different set of persons, one beyond recognition. He still felt something, but it wasn't how he used to feel, and this left him frustrated and confused.

The evening could have ended in one of two ways – the four of them could have decided to throw every last bit of decorum to the wind and retreated to a hotel suite suitable for four, or one of them could have thrown a punch and started a mêlée. Neither of these scenarios took place; the lack of drama was, perversely, subtly dramatic—a tableau of unresolved tension.

Out on the street, they shook hands and kissed and said goodnight. Marc wondered what he would say to Paul the next time they were at work together, and Max wondered if he'd ever see Django Bernhardt again.

The next day, Marc felt compelled to write to Sarah. His recent sequence of unforced associations ended up creating a soupçon of guilt.

25 April 1919

My dear Sarah,

I do hope you are well. I haven't written to you in a while, so I thought to take this moment to take pen to hand at last.

I have been busier than I ever expected to be. It turns out peace is just as consequential as war when it comes to helping and healing. There are fewer wounded men now, but many more cases of pneumonia due to influenza. Because of this, I'm still at the hospital six days a week, although the work lets up enough every now and then long enough for me to take a walk the park and go out for dinner or drinks with my colleagues.

My social life, such as it is, consists mainly of outings with my best friend here, the British doctor I told you about, Paul Cordette. He knows Paris like a native, and he's brought me to all sorts of bohemian places. You'd wonder to see me watching poetry recited on the Left Bank or downing emerald-colored cocktails at a café on the Île de France. Paul is higher up in the ranks than I am, and party to more up-to-date information. He thinks most of our work will be done by the end of next month. If that comes true, I can wrap things up here and be back in Louisville by July.

I hope you are well and keeping out of mischief. I miss you and think of you often. Even though I am no longer in harm's way, I hope you will continue to keep me in your prayers, as I keep you in mine.

With love, Marc

Marc knew his letter was mostly lies, but he did not know how to put the truth about what was happening to him in words, especially to someone so distant in miles and memory. In fact, he did not know how to tell the truth at all, because he wasn't sure what the truth was. Marc felt suspended in the air—he loved what he remembered of Sarah, and he loved what he had with Aurélie and with Marc; in fact, in the latter cases, he didn't even know if he loved one of them more than the other.

But, a few days later, before he could begin to figure any of this out, a letter came from Sarah.

28 April 1919

Darling Marcus,

It's been a long while, I know, but at last, I have real news to write about: I am coming to France!

I know how busy you are and how dedicated you are to your work, and I've grown weary of merely supporting you from afar. I've booked passage for myself on the La Touraine; we sail from Newport News on the 5th and dock at Le Havre on the 13th. I should arrive in Paris the next day—two weeks from today, two weeks until I can hold you in my arms once more, my darling. Isn't this the best of the turning of the tides?

I'll likely be underway by the time this letter reaches you, so don't bother to write back. Just utter a 'bon voyage' in your prayers and keep me in your dreams.

I can't wait.

All my love, Sarah

Their letters had crossed. Sarah Gold was going to be in Paris in two weeks.

IX

Pierre

Pierre Laprix was no fool; he knew many of his fellow deputies humored him and were waiting for him to die so that they could replace him with someone more aligned with their conservative positions. This, perversely, enhanced his reputation for integrity amongst his constituents. The opposition called it stubbornness, but it allowed him to be reelected over and over again.

Pierre was a long-standing and unrepentant liberal: he supported Dreyfuss and opposed Maurras; he attended church but refused to allow the clergy to dictate the law, and he would stand for an hour in the *Chambre* **des députés** and speak in defense of a bill doomed to defeat in order to have his point of view entered into the record.

He was born in Charleville, a forested town near the Belgian border; his childhood familiarity with the long country roads and the deep, secluded woods stood him well for his future choice of a career. It taught him to value permanence and to respect the natural order—two pillars of existence that disintegrated with the Franco-Prussian war. His boyhood hometown was overrun twice—first by the Germans, and then by the French. Very little worth keeping remained, his person included.

When Pierre turned twenty, he moved to Paris and began his career in business and politics. He left his battle-scarred, provincial youth behind; he established his own manufactory by the turn of the century, and shortly after that he was elected as a deputy in the Chambre for the first of his so-far four terms. Monsieur Laprix cultivated the image of a serious, committed, and, frankly, boringly idealistic politician. He stayed away from the nightclubs; he refused most social invitations, and he spent most of his evenings reading the papers, or Montaigne, or anything at all that extended his erudition at the expense of nearly everything else. And then he met Aurélie Beauchamps.

It happened on a warm summer night in 1906 at a party being held at a ministry on the Quai d'Orsay in honor of the American ambassador—not quite a ball, but more than a mere hour of cocktails. The deshabille caused by the weather allowed for a certain amount of informality, and Gabrielle Sternberk was just brazened enough to instigate the match. By then, of course, she was Aurélie's lover, and she knew Pierre Laprix well enough to have escorted him three times when an even number was needed. Because of this, no formal introductions were necessary; she took Pierre's left hand, and Aurélie's right hand, and entwined them, and a host of potential problems were solved.

The marriage of Pierre Laprix to Aurélie Beauchamps took all of social Paris by surprise, not the least being the principal parties involved. Pierre was forty-six; he had given up the idea of a wife decades ago and had practically given up on love entirely. It just didn't seem like something he had time for. Mademoiselle Beauchamps, on the other hand, at twenty-five had already experienced enough loving attachments to sustain an ordinary person's lifetime. She had nearly a full decade of balls, courtiers, lovers, affairs, and scandals behind her. No one thought their relationship would last a month, let alone a lifetime, but they were wrong.

Their special bond was advanced the night Pierre escorted Aurélie to a ball at the Luxembourg Palace. Aurélie pretended to be dazzled by the extravagance of the gowns and the richness of the food, and Pierre hid his distaste for the diversions of the upper classes in order to impress his date. When the two of them had the chance for a frank conversation on a bench in the garden at midnight and discovered their shared sense of amusement at the whole of it, their future together was sealed.

The engagement was announced a fortnight later; the night before the announcement, Aurélie filled Pierre in on what, exactly, she liked to do with Gabrielle Sternberk and, furthermore, how much she would wish to continue to do it. Pierre, being liberal in his personal beliefs as much as his politics, supported her absolutely. For a man who actually disliked the act of making love and much preferred banter, good wine, and a long novel, the revelation that he could gain the status of a happily married man without any of the private responsibilities that came with such a position pleased him immensely.

By cultivating Pierre Laprix's affection, Aurélie instantly gained access to all the most important dinner parties and every possible social environment without having to go through the bother of seducing an inappropriate partner and thus be forced to keep quiet about it. All anyone cared about was that she was respectably married; after that, she could be sleeping with a horse and no one would care.

And by marrying Aurélie Beauchamps, Pierre would not only become the legal heir to the Beauchamps fortune but a man escorting a legendary beauty, the kind of beauty that illuminates everything in view and smooths the path of anyone entering the world of politics.

More than a decade had passed since. Aurélie proved as steadfast across time as she had that first night at the ministry. She had other, smaller affairs, of course, little liaisons that were like ripples on an otherwise placid pond. Most of them were with older men, who were less likely to make unreasonable demands; among them there was a retired army officer with one arm and a fondness for riding crops, and a sommelier whose primary attribute was his access to vintage bottles of Lafite-Rothschild.

Every now and then, Aurélie would form a longer attachment, one that lasted months as opposed to weeks or days. Most prominent amongst these affairs was a lengthy partnering with a British captain; he was twenty-two, she was thirty-three. Between the two of them they had the stamina to last through at least a half-dozen hotel rooms, a long weekend in Reims, the usual spring floods, and a summer heat wave, all while dodging the usual impediments caused by an extremely inconvenient war. Pierre remained behind the curtain throughout, an indifferently amused spectator.

And then Aurélie Laprix met Marcus Greenspan.

Pierre wasn't sure what to make of the latest squire to conquer Aurélie's heart. First of all, he wasn't at all certain if Marc had made a conquest at all; usually, the man or the woman would be like a fly to a spider, trapped. Pierre was used to Aurélie setting the terms of the affair and consulting Pierre along the way as if he were her manager and not her husband, but something about this new young man was different.

Aurélie seemed genuinely impressed by Marc and willing to tolerate his youth for much longer than was strictly necessary. Most of all, he was an American; in their twelve years together, Pierre couldn't recall a single lover from outside Aurélie's continental circle, and here was one from across an ocean. Not only that, but Americans, as Germany had learned over the past year, do not give up easily.

Pierre's solution was to ask for a meeting. It was well enough to see his latest adversary in the flesh once, and before things turned serious; after all, he was there when Marc and Aurélie first met that cold night in January. But three months had passed; the bitter winter had turned into a promising spring, and with it, a blossoming of Aurélie's relations with Marc that put it, in Pierre's books, as nearly equal to, and thus as deserving of his attention, as her relations with Miss Sternberk. He reserved a table for three at a charming little bistro in the Passages du Panoramas for a Saturday evening in early May, and let his wife take care of issuing the invitations.

When the day arrived, Pierre played the perfect gentleman and allowed Aurélie and Marc to arrive first. He knew by doing this he was giving them the advantage; they could, if they wished, even rehearse their conversation as if it was the opening act of a play, but he also knew that giving his wife the opportunity to relax would leave her and her beaux in a more unguarded state and thus easier to parse.

"Good evening, Monsieur Greenspan," Pierre said, removing his hat and hanging it on a rack next to the door.

"Sir." Marc stood and clasped Pierre's hand. It was the greeting of two colleagues, a negotiation of presumed equals very much like the one going on between the victorious nations at that very moment inside the palace at Versailles. Pierre had put on one of his best suits, light brown linen with faint gold stripes. Both Marc and Aurélie were ever so slightly more casually dressed—he in a white linen shirt and red bowtie; she in a pair of Egyptian cotton knickers with silk trim.

"Have you had a chance to look at the menu?" Pierre asked. It was often this way with Pierre, to blithely deflect from the matter at hand.

"Not yet," Marc replied. "We were naturally waiting for you."

"Naturally."

Aurélie thought there was a slight tinge of sarcasm to Pierre's tone, but she chose to let it pass.

"I hear the veal is quite good," Marc said.

"I'll have the bouillabaisse," Aurélie said. Marc was used to Aurélie ordering anything other than what was recommended, but he wondered if she was making an especial case for independence due to Pierre's company.

"The veal for me," Pierre added. "And how about a bottle of Veuve Clicquot?"

"Excellent."

So far, their meal held all the qualities of a high-toned business luncheon. Marc thought that at any moment, the two Laprixs would start discussing something related to an inventory, and he wondered if it were up to him to choose a topic. On her part, Aurélie wished Gabrielle was there to at least make it four and help equalize things. Pierre looked for all the world like he was waiting for the bill from the moment he sat down.

It took the mention of Maximilian Berger to break the ice.

"How is Max these days?" Aurélie asked.

Marc was wondering why Aurélie chose, in the presence of her husband and her lover, to bring up her lover's other lover. It was, at the very least, provocative, and perhaps also beside the point, as he had assumed Pierre knew as much about his goings-on as he knew about Pierre—meaning everything.

"I think he's well," Marc replied. "I saw him on Thursday."

"I cannot help but comment on the novelty of our situation," Pierre began. He paused as the waiter showed up with the wine and the stand and uncorked it and poured. When the sommelier moved too far away to overhear the conversation, he continued: "I've grown used to my dear wife's escapades, and I've had the chance to dine with many of her beaux across the years. But I do believe this is the first time that one of Aurélie's lovers has a lover of his own, and a young man at that."

"Would it suit you better if he was sleeping with an old man?" Aurélie asked. "Marc, why don't you fall in love with one of those mustachioed veterans who fought in Indochina? That way, in company, he and my husband could spend the time conversing about the utility of sampans."

"Don't be brittle, my dear," Pierre said. "I was being matter of fact, not sarcastic."

"I suppose the circumstances are unusual," Marc said. "Did Aurélie happen to mention I have a fiancé back in America?"

"Oh, ho." Pierre let out a laugh that was loud enough to be noticed at the next table. Aurélie was startled; she never recalled hearing her husband laugh so publicly before. "Are you deliberately trying to make your life as complicated as possible?"

"Yes, sir," Marc replied. "I'm a voracious complicator."

"You're a voracious something," Aurélie added.

Their meals arrived: two fish stews and one veal. Marc took advantage of the pause to steer the conversation towards a slightly different port.

"I'm quite capable of being philosophical about what is happening to me, Monsieur Laprix," he began. "The war did that. Before I came over to help, I bought in to the 'one life, one direction' ideal. I thought I would age well, like this wine, growing better with each year. I would gather up, in turn, a medical degree, some practical experience, a wife and a home, and a son and a daughter."

"One of each, a perfect plan," Aurélie said.

"But here I was thrown into an experience that changed everything. I mean, I expected the war to change me, but I had no idea of how. And then I met Madame Laprix, and Max Berger. Suddenly—or maybe not so suddenly, more like ink on a blotter, slowly spreading—my convictions were undermined. In the end, I no longer believed in my own doctrine. May I speak frankly?"

"My boy, haven't we been frank enough already?" Pierre asked. "You're sleeping with my wife, and with a German soldier, all while keeping a Southern belle in waiting back home. I can't imagine there's any frankness missing from that equation."

"I meant, I would like to try, for my own reasons as well as to please you, to try to talk truthfully about what has happened to me since I met Aurélie."

"Have you not spoken truthfully to us so far, Marc?" Aurélie asked.

"Yes. I meant I have behaved truthfully, but I don't think I have spoken about it to you, or to anyone."

"Proceed." Pierre made a grand gesture, as if inviting Marc into an interview.

"My first thought was of fairness," Marc said. "To be fair, most of all, to you, sir, as you are deserving of the whole of my respect. And then to be fair to your wife, not to deceive her with Max, or make her feel any less loved by me because of him. And, lastly, to be fair to myself – to not cheat myself out of any emotion, including those which, conversely, might make me less fair. It's been a breathtaking trip for me."

"Well, come up for air," Pierre said, laughing. "And have a spoonful of your bouillabaisse. If you truly believe in fairness, letting it get cold would be unfair to the chef."

Aurélie claimed the floor.

"I'm glad you see your position in all this as one of fairness," she began. "But I am more experienced in love, and I know that love is something that almost never plays fair."

"Life itself doesn't play fair," Pierre added. "And I've lived longer than the both of you, so you know I don't say that frivolously."

"I'm impressed by your sophistication, sir," Marc said. "To be honest, if I found myself in a situation like this in Kentucky, I'd either be tarred and feathered by the citizenry or driven out of town by a gang with pitchforks."

"You are in Paris, not Kentucky," Aurélie said.

"And what of Kentucky?" Pierre asked. "I assume, in lieu of what you have just told us, that you haven't mentioned a word of this to your fiancé."

"You are correct," Marc said. "And furthermore, she is coming to see me. She'll be here in barely a week."

"*Alors!*" Aurélie said. "And when were you going to tell me this news?"

"I just got her letter yesterday," Marc said. "She's half-way across the Atlantic by now. I thought of sending a telegram to her ship, but that's not really the best way to tell someone you're having an affair."

"I'll be easier to explain than Max," Aurélie said. "Some girls I know are a little uneasy when they find out their boyfriend is having an affair with a man, even if it is in Paris."

"None of it will be easy," Marc said. "I've got to be responsible, but that's as difficult to parse as 'fair'. There's no way I can be fair to everyone, is there?"

"Then I guess, in the end, you'll have to do what's fair for yourself, and let the chips fall where they may," Pierre said. "In the meantime, we must discuss a considerably more important matter. Who wants the *éclair du chocolat?*"

Aurélie countered her dinner with Pierre and Marc by running to Gabrielle's arms. It was a safe and secure redoubt; after all, Aurélie's relationship with Gabrielle had lasted longer than the one with her husband, and was more like a conventional marriage, too, with the partners relying on parrying banter, common interests, and a solid circle of like-mined friends who support them. It was, shockingly, the most bourgeois thing about it.

Gabrielle provoked a conversation with Aurélie about the *bourgeoisie* aspect of their relationship over an extravagant tea in the dining room of the Hotel Ritz. The hotel was spectacularly overbooked due to the Peace Conference, and while some measure of calm could be found in the restaurant, the lobby was overrun. Men in formal wear and women with tiaras and gowns flowed in and out; several of them were heads of state and quite a few were also royalty. The whole of it gave Aurélie and Gabrielle's time together there the aura of a fairytale; it could only have been improved upon if they had arrived at the hotel in a horse-drawn carriage.

"What do you imagine is the future of your relationship with Marc and Pierre?" Gabrielle asked. Between the two of them, they had split two pots of tea, a pair of smoked salmon sandwiches, a cream scone, and a slice of bourbon pie. "Have you assigned each of them a specific role, with percentages?"

"You sound like my solicitor, Gaby," Aurélie said.

"If I were your solicitor, I'd be advising you to simplify," Gabrielle replied. "Lovers, like bank accounts, can fail to draw interest if they're neglected."

"That's quite clever. Is it you who feels neglected, my darling?"

"Me, no, not in the slightest. I was only thinking of Marc and Pierre."

"The men in my life, as I suppose *La vie Parisienne* would put it."

"Precisely."

"Well, as you know, in the past my escape plan was always to find a new lover," Aurélie said. "This was more easily obtained in my youth. Now, of necessity, I've had to narrow my focus, and I functionally have two lovers, one of each sex. I'm not sure what you mean, then, by 'neglected'."

"I'm not only counting the hours, Aury. I know Pierre has gotten over his expectations, but I'm afraid poor Marc is only just beginning to catalogue them. What will you do when he wants to keep you for himself, or—*quelle horreur*—wishes to whisk you away to America?"

"Marc hasn't suggested either of those possibilities."

"Yet. But the clock is ticking. You booted out that Spanish diplomat after a month, and I believe your affair with the daughter of the Countess d' Auxerre made it all the way through a season. Sooner or later, Marc is going to want some kind of reward for his patience."

"Wasn't it you who told me, a decade ago, that my love was all the reward you'd need?"

"Yes, but I'm not an American doctor. I'm French. I was raised to be impractical."

"Now you're just being flighty," Aurélie said. "Why don't you just tell me what you want me to do? Wouldn't that be so much easier?"

"Much easier, my dear," Gabrielle replied. "But so much less fun."

In the end, it was Pierre Laprix who suggested the basis for continuance that all the parties would agree to, even if some of them would remain temporarily ignorant of the plan. After all, Aurélie might be the heiress to the Beauchamps fortune and the status it brought, and Gabrielle the steering mechanism to it, but it was the men—Pierre, in consort with Marc and Max—who were the more practical experts in its application, especially as applied to the cost of social comforts in Paris in the spring of 1919. Each of them deftly held to the illusion they held some influence over the situation.

Pierre laid it all out for Aurélie one morning over breakfast. He usually found the first meal of the day to be the best time to approach his wife with anything resembling a hurdle, before resistance in the form of a sharp parasol or an application for a credit account could be produced. The two of them were seated in the ruins of the meal, a half-buttered croissant here, a coffee-stained cup there.

"I've freshened your accounts for June," Pierre began. "But if you don't mind, now that dining in plein air is more possible, perhaps you could take your luncheons in one of the parks."

This was Pierre's exquisitely subtle way to telling his wife that the hotel bills for her assignations with Marc needed to be tempered. It was an efficiency she had been assigned in the past, and it was not an unreasonable one. But then Pierre went on to extend his purview beyond his usual myopia.

"I'd like to help Marcus Greenspan more."

Aurélie suspected Pierre helping Marc meant something different from her helping Marc, but she had to test the waters, so to speak, before jumping in.

"What, precisely, do you mean, Pierre?"

"From what I have observed, his household, so to speak, is in more need of support than our own. There's that young man of his…"

"Max Berger."

"Yes, that is his name. A poor Alsatian boy in the big city. I might take pity."

"Are you really that interested in the prospects of Max Berger?"

"You surmised correctly."

"So that if Marc spends more time with Max, he will concurrently spend less time with me?"

"That is an adjacent accomplishment, I must admit."

"Adjacent or direct, my dear, it is still more of an interference than you usually commit. Why do you feel this way?"

"Don't fret, Aurélie," Pierre began. "This is purely a matter of affinity. In the admittedly brief amount of time that I have thought about it, I see a vastly larger potential for happiness for the two of them than I do with Marc and you, or Max and anybody else, for that matter."

"So you rank their happiness—and your own—above mine?"

"Question upon question, Aurélie. Now I may posit one of my own: when I have ever not given primary consideration to your happiness?"

"Until now, never."

"Are you really happy with Marc?"

"He amuses me."

"He's not a toy, Aurélie. He's a grown man. With a sturdy German boy for company and a fiancé in America. Dabble all you like, but I still think you'd be better breaking it off or slowing it down. If I could, I would like to have some measure of control over the situation from afar. My part in this will be, as I suggested, an endowment."

"From my estate? That's cruel."

"I can provide the funds. You will provide the emotional support. That is how the two of us, serving as benevolent patrons, will help the romance of Dr. Greenspan and Jäger Berger extend into a new chapter."

Pierre stood up and nodded in the direction of the kitchen.

"Now, my darling, would you like half a grapefruit?"

X

Paul

Paul Cordette always knew he wanted to be a doctor. His fascination with the human body began when he was in the First Form at a boarding school in Yorkshire. He was ten years old, and there was a boy's changing room behind the gymnasium. Being the only son of Marie and Francis Cordette, it was his first chance to see other boys without their clothes on. It made an impression.

Paul wondered, *how do these magnificent contraptions work, and how can I grow up to work on them?* He thought that boy's bodies were like machines, needing spare parts and careful maintenance in order to keep functioning. Thus were his profession and his sexual proclivities forever linked.

As Paul matured, his view of his prospects remained not that far from ordinary if your family was upper middle-class with the usual aspirations. He breezed through secondary school and college, and he spent two years at Cambridge earning his medical degree and promulgating a series of amatory relationships.

Among his lovers, Paul counted the Dean's youngest son, a freckle-faced redhead with an aptitude for athletic fornication, and the keeper at his house's pool—an eager lad named Freddie who liked skimpy bathing suits and taught Paul foreign words like frottage and fellatio. Paul never counted any of these relationships as permanent because he couldn't consider it possible. He believed men like him never stayed with their partners for very long.

What was possible was a career in medicine. After Cambridge, there was an internship at a hospital in Birmingham, followed by a blissful summer as a laboratory assistant in Bremen. There, Paul perfected his German, learned continental methods of suturing, and added a string of gorgeous and willing blonds to his inventory of conquests. All the while, Francis and Marie started to give up wondering when their oldest and most ambitious child might finally settle down, even after they realized the settling down might be with another man.

And just when all the branches of the Cordette family had stopped thinking about Paul's future relations, the good doctor fell in love. Paul had worked very hard at not allowing this to happen, thinking any party he engaged in a tryst must be damaged if they considered him to be quality goods worth keeping, but something about Michael Ashenden triggered an avalanche of feelings that included several new ones such as permanency, domestication, and security. That fact that it was entirely unexpected made Paul feel even more like it was part of a waking dream.

The two men met at a coffee shop in Whitechapel in the spring of 1914; Paul was pulling a shift at the Royal London Hospital and Michael was a chimney sweep on a work break. They sat side by side, struck up a conversation, and discovered—simply, and with hardly any effort at all—that some form of sexual energy flowed between them. When Michael asked if Paul had the time, Paul pulled his watch out of his pocket and smiled, and then offered to give up an hour or two of it if Michael was willing. The two of them walked over to Paul's flat in Bethnal Green.

The Ashenden boy was quite unlike anyone Paul had ever slept with. First off, Michael was an actual boy—seventeen years-old (Paul was twenty-five at the time). In addition, Michael was, relatively speaking, uneducated—no Oxbridge for this working-class son. But, most importantly, Michael truly loved Paul; the sex, while fun and fulfilling, was right from the start secondary to his admiration of and dedication to his new friend. And Paul felt the same way about Michael.

Until Paul Cordette met Michael Ashenden, he thought he was doomed to a life of secret encounters and mismatched emotions. All his previous relationships had either ended before they could really begin due to the strain that society would place on them had the truth ever come to light, or, if a large enough circle of friends was found to include them, the tenderness Paul felt would dissipate into jealousy, or dissatisfaction, or just plain incompatibility. With Michael, all that faded in the face of apparent perfection.

After a month, Paul asked Michael to come and live with him; they started to share not only a bed but all their meals and most of their free time. The city of London became their picnic ground. Paul even offered to support Michael if he chose to stop sweeping chimneys and wanted to do something different, like paint or learn a musical instrument. Their future together shone like a clear, blue dawn.

Then the archduke was assassinated in Sarajevo, ultimatums were issued, and suddenly Britain was swept into a war. Medical officers, especially unmarried medical officers such as Paul Cordette, were desperately needed in Belgium. Michael was too young to serve, and even if he had been old enough to join up, he would have to go through months of training in some horrible place like Aldershot or Salisbury. The two lovers thought about ignoring the world—after all, the world had ignored their type for eons—but the price was too high. If Paul chose to act so precipitously, he would have to consider the immorality of turning his back on his fellow man.

In the end, Paul volunteered; there was a tearful farewell at the Whitechapel Station. In order to assuage his heartbreak, Paul wrote frequent letters to Michael where he documented, in unashamed detail, all the things he wanted to do with him once they could be together again. Michael was a less prolific but equally eager correspondent. Their letters to each other flowed back and forth, but stagnation set in and the time drifted away. Paul knew himself well enough to think he hadn't changed very much, but he had no idea how Michael felt at all.

Finally, Paul got leave to return to London for ten days over Christmas. He hardly spent a moment of the first five of those days apart from Michael's arms. Paul had kept his flat; they stayed in bed and sent up for sandwiches and beer. Paul felt that if he left Michael's side for even ten minutes, their separation would become permanent; it held the form of a premonition.

Unfortunately, the premonition turned out to be true: on an otherwise ordinary Saturday afternoon, midway through Paul's leave, Michael Ashenden went out to get a paper and some fish and chips while Paul decided it was time for tidying up.

On his way home, Michael caught his cuff on a bicycle parked in the gutter on the corner of St James Avenue and Old Ford Road. He slipped on a patch of ice and fell into the path of an omnibus. The bus didn't have enough time to brake, and Michael received a fatal head wound. The war had produced a death in the family, after all, only not in the manner in which Paul had expected. The end was always meant to be his own. Fate, he discovered, could be both bitter and ironic.

There was a funeral two days later in St. Dunstan's in Stepney, in the same chapel where Michael was christened. Michael's parents mourned their son and buried him and never paid any attention to the tear-stricken officer standing in the back of the chapel. Suddenly, the world was topsy-turvy: London was a place of siege, and the trenches in France felt like home. Paul packed up his kit and recrossed the Channel, vowing to never, ever fall in love again.

The scenes that greeted Paul on the Western Front in the spring of 1915 matched his misanthropic mood; it was as terrible a landscape as he had ever seen. He jumped from Saint Quentin to Arras to Neuve Chapelle, trying to put pieces of men back together and failing miserably most of the time. Twice, Paul was in the direct path of a shell; he was spared only because the soldier on top of him was dead. The flow of wounded men was like a tidal pool and Paul could barely distinguish between the dead and the living; at times, he wasn't even sure which side of that great divide he was on. *If I die,* he thought, *at least I will be reunited with my beloved Michael.*

But Paul Cordette didn't die in the war; almost against his will, he thrived. He served as the chief medical officer for an entire British brigade, and then, when his term of service was up, he was brought in to run the recovery wards at the American Hospital in Paris. He rented a suite of rooms in Batignolles, took up watercolor painting, and prowled the boulevards for company.

This pattern—which really wasn't a pattern at all, but mostly an empty series of successive gestures that filled a desperate need for a direction that might never come—lasted for two years. The war kept going, but Paul was weary of it. He was about to give up on Paris and return to something in London— he didn't know what—when Marcus Greenspan was assigned to his hospital ward.

Paul thought Marc was cute. Through conversations across their time working together, he had learned that Marc was engaged to be married, but that fact didn't prevent Paul from fantasizing about him. Paul held a specific image in mind when he did so—Marc in his uniform, the few dark chest hairs poking out of the top of his shirt, the stubble on Marc's cheek after a skipped day of shaving, the slender muscles tensing on Marc's biceps.

As the war wound down, Paul started to wonder about how far to pursue his friendship with this eager but enigmatic American. Something in that young man's eyes offered an invitation. If he ever got to be alone with Marc, would he have a chance?

The chance, when it came, was on a rainy night around Christmas. The war had been over for a month, and the organization of the hospital was in an uproar, with people resigning or requesting reassignment and patients and prisoners changing their status from day to day. Marc was performing rounds on the French ward that day, and Paul was in charge. At five o'clock, Paul dismissed the staff (except for the night nurse) and locked the door, and he and Marc walked down to the boulevard Victor-Hugo for some hot chocolate.

The two men were sitting side by side at the counter when Paul accidentally bumped his arm against Marc's, spilling a large splash of the cocoa on Paul's trousers. Without thinking much about it, Marc grabbed his napkin and used it to blot up as much of the stain as he could. Paul stared at Marc as Marc rubbed his clothed hand up and down over and over Paul's thigh. *He has no idea what's he's doing to me,* Paul thought, at the same time hoping against hope that some sort of spark would ignite in his friend's mind. Paul was on the verge of reaching over and petting Marc's leg and letting the chips fall where they may, but he resisted and allowed the chance to pass him by.

Something might have come of it, but then Maximilian Berger arrived on the ward. Marc's behavior towards Paul changed; he put it down at first to war weariness, and then, possibly, to boredom with his friendship. It took close observation, but not too much insinuation, to discover Max's sexual preferences and Marc's itinerant interest, and—a little later, after Max was released—to hear from Marc's own ears proof of their joint attraction.

When Paul discovered that Marc was a homosexual—despite the overwhelming evidence to the contrary provided by his engagement to Sarah Gold, let alone his ongoing affair with Aurélie Laprix—he altered his view of his friend. Paul no longer thought of Marc as quarry, but as an ally. He was thrilled by their lightly shared secret and almost immediately assigned Marc the role of best friend; he had never had a male companion who wasn't a bed partner. This new equation continued through March and into April. The fantasies remained, but the smoldering embers of attraction were doused by the springs of companionship. Then Paul Cordette fell for Django Bernhardt.

It began, as affairs often do, in complete innocence. By

basking in his colleague's newfound affinity, Paul discovered his need for a sexual companion was at least moderately diminished. He stopped wandering over to Montmartre or walking along the boulevard Saint-Germain two or three nights a week, choosing instead to hang out with Marc and Max, or Marc and Aurélie, or—*quelle scandale!*—just Marc. Every now and then when in need of mild amusement, Paul would walk along the Seine and look at the fairy lights strung along the *bateaux mouches* there.

One night in April, Paul turned in from the river and stopped at a bench in the Jardin des Plantes. The air was cool and clear, and with it came a feeling of clarity: *this is my life now – I help people during the day, and I help myself in the evening, and my colleague (who is also my friend) is symbolically holding my hand the whole of the way.* It was a rested feeling, and it made Paul sleepy. He closed his eyes and listened to the ordinary city sounds surrounding him: a car horn, a lovers' quarrel in an unrecognizable language, a bird singing in a tree.

When Paul opened his eyes, there was a young man sitting on the bench next to him.

"Good evening," the man said. Paul was startled, but only for an instant.

"*Bon soir*," Paul said.

At first, Paul didn't recognize the man, but then he heard the German accent, and the pieces fell into place. Paris is a big city, but apparently not that big.

"You are Maximilian Berger's friend, from the American Hospital, are you not?" Paul asked.

"I am...I was..."

"I am a doctor there."

"Yes. I remember," Django said. To cover for his wondering just how much he should say about Max or anything, he took out a pack of cigarettes from his jacket pocket and offered one to Paul.

"Would you like one?" he asked.

"No, thank you. But allow me."

Paul took out his silver cigarette lighter and held the flame in front of Django's face. He knew that lighting another man's cigarette was one of the coded gestures used to signal an interest.

"*Danke,*" Django said. "Or should I say *merci?*"

"As you prefer. 'Thanks' would also be fine."

Django drew in a breath and let out some smoke. Then he spoke:

"My name is Django."

"I remember," Paul said. "And you might know me as Dr. Cordette, but please call me Paul." Paul thought that the moment called for a cigarette after all, so he took one out and lit it. "Django—that's a very unusual name."

"Not to me. It's a gypsy name, although my mother and father were far from being gypsies. I never knew why they chose it for me, but now it belongs to me as much as my skin."

"It's a very nice name," Paul said. "And you've very nice skin." Paul reached out and put his hand on Django's chin. "Would you like to have a drink with me?"

"Yes, I'd like that very much."

Paul and Django walked towards the place de la Concorde. They stopped at a bar Paul knew and had gin fizzes, and then Paul called a cab and they went back to Paul's flat in Batignolles.

To Paul, Django's lovemaking was as exotic as his name. The young man wasn't evincing any of the things that Paul expected in a first encounter—purpose, curiosity, the usual patter to fill in the gaps. Instead, Django behaved like he had known Paul—and loved Paul—forever. He languished and rolled around and changed positions like a lazy puppy. And—also like a puppy—he acted like everything they were doing was new.

Paul sensed that Django was an inexperienced lover; he was shy and hesitant. In that sense, the two men were well-matched – Paul liked to play Vergil—and their time together in bed was thus colored with the thrilling sense of equilibrium that can arise between a master and his pupil.

Afterwards, Django mentioned something about a room near the Gare de l'Est, but Paul convinced him to stay the night. At some point while they were lying in bed together, Django filled Paul in on his childhood in Colmar, his ineffectual years of service during the war, and, as a form of confession, the details of the beginning and the end of his romance with Maximilian Berger. The past was clearly the past.

Paul met Django again two days later for dinner at a restaurant near the Tuileries, followed by another night of lovemaking. It was early in their affair, and although they were both happy about what had happened so far, neither one of them thought anything at all about context. There was as yet little need for the building blocks that turn brief encounters into some form of permanence with an expansion of their relations into the public area of friends and colleagues.

But then, the day after that, Paul and Django went to Pick's, and saw Marc and Max (and Gabrielle and Aurélie), and the kaleidoscope that was their lives made one more dazzling and unpredictable turn.

XI

Gabrielle

Gabrielle and Aurélie were having breakfast in the Hotel Madeleine Plaza. They were debating, once again, the terms of their continuance—an invisible contract in constant need of amending. Gabrielle wished to raise an objection.

"We have two perfectly good houses between us, both with excellent addresses," she said. "I don't see why you need to entertain Marc in chic cafés and expensive hotel rooms."

"I haven't ever heard you complain about the cost of things before," Aurélie began. She passed up the chance to point out the irony of her friend's statement, as it was issued in one of Paris' most expensive dining rooms. "Are you jealous, my darling?"

Gabrielle took a sip of her coffee, and pushed her omelet around the plate, hoping the brief delay in the conversation would help her find the right words to say.

"I am younger than you, Aury, but I'm still too old to play that game. I got over being jealous of your love affairs a decade ago. I was merely suggesting that you and Marc might be happier in a domestic setting."

"What, and have him come into the drawing room in his slippers and ask where we keep the sugar?"

"You make a dramatic point of it, but yes—I don't see why we can't all just be grown-up about it. And my house would do just as well as yours, although I suppose Dr. Greenspan would feel a little put out if I was lingering in the hallway while the two of you dressed."

"And what would I do with Pierre at home?" Aurélie asked. "Stash him in a walk-in closet until Marc gets his things together?"

The garçon came by with the coffee urn and poured them both another cup.

"Now you're just being ridiculous, Aury," Gabrielle replied. "Your house has enough rooms to accommodate half a dozen suitors directly under your husband's nose. For all I know, it has already done so in the past. You rush away from dinner with Pierre to meet Marc at the Opéra; I hire a taxi to take me from shopping on the rue Royale to meet you at a lesbian bar in Montmartre. All this sneaking about is taking the shape of a bad bedroom farce, and it should be beyond our dignity by now."

"I hadn't imagined the possibility of anything being beyond your dignity, Gaby," Aurélie said. "When you first told me of your dissatisfaction, I was expecting you to propose an orgy."

"Orgies are fine when they're arranged. Spontaneity is fine when it's under control. I don't object to your activities; it's the haphazardness of it all that keeps me on edge."

"Fine," Aurélie said, punctuating her remark with a forkful of the last bits of her eggs. "We'll throw a party. I'll install Pierre in our boudoir, Marc can have the guest suite, and you can troll Montmartre for someone to keep for yourself in the parlor. Surely my chaise longue can fit two."

"Don't be brittle," Gabrielle said. "But as a matter of fact, a party's not a bad idea. It might add a bit of social leavening to our currently half-baked affairs. Do invite Marc's friend, the German boy...what's his name?"

"Max."

"Max, yes. And check in with Pierre and see if he's had any interesting affairs lately," Gabrielle said. "I can fill out the guest list with some of my acquaintances at *Le Monocle*."

"Pierre never has affairs anymore, interesting or otherwise," Aurélie said. "I think he's bored. The other day he made the ridiculous suggestion of giving Max some kind of annuity, like he was our ward. Pierre is free to do what he wants with his money, of course, but I hardly think of supporting former prisoners of war as a suitable charity. I have no idea what he's up to."

"Never mind that," Gabrielle said. "Who else should we invite?"

"Well, certainly Pierre knows of a baron or two who appreciates men—or women, for that matter, or both—and might like the distraction. Plus, there must be one or two unmarried deputies."

"What does it matter if they're married or not? As long as they're handsome."

"You started this conversation with a complaint about not staying at home and ended it by suggesting a ball."

"There are ballrooms for balls," Gabrielle said. "What I have in mind is merely a slightly scandalous soirée. You haven't brought out the Limoges in a while. Frankly, I think it's the best idea I've come up with in months."

"Very well. Let me check Pierre's calendar," Aurélie said. "I don't want to schedule something and then find out he's supposed to be on an inspection tour in the Sedan."

"Make it soon," Gabrielle said. "You never know when the bloom will fall off the rose."

"Is that a threat, my dear?"

"I was thinking of Marcus Greenspan, but if you wish, you may call it a threat," Gabriella replied. She put on her hat. "I merely consider it an observation."

The party was planned for the second Saturday in May. Gabrielle nearly went straight from her breakfast with Aurélie to the printers—Pierre's approbation be damned—and the invitations were delivered with a week to spare. Propriety dictated that Pierre and Aurélie Laprix served as hosts, although everyone understood it was Gabrielle Sternberk who was behind the scheme. There was no R.S.V.P because there wasn't enough time, and, regardless, no one in their right mind rejects an invitation of any kind from the Laprixs.

The guests included Marc and Max, of course, but also Paul

and Django, Pierre's bachelor deputies, and two of Gabrielle's former lovers—a woman named Daphne who was married to an American businessman from Duluth but ditched him within a week of arriving in Paris, and a Belgian courtesan in her fifties who liked cigars and horses. Aurélie convinced Gabrielle to invite a pair of female dancers from Pick's who were young enough to be pliant and would make the seating arrangements neater.

Twelve was a good number—not too many to leave a wallflower or two standing on the periphery of the room, but enough to guarantee at least four decent conversations over the course of the night. There had been problems in the past when there were too many guests and everyone felt slighted by the hostess' lack of attention, or too few, leaving Aurélie with the unpleasant task of having to talk to bores.

"Welcome!" Aurélie shouted as people started to show up. She had to shout because the band had been installed in front of the parlor fountain; there were only four musicians, but ragtime is loud and the walls echoed a bit. Introductions were made all around. There was enough food to require the guests to survey the tables for at least half an hour before beginning to make their selections.

Marc and Max and Paul and Django were last to arrive; this was not planned as a dramatic gesture or even a deliberate faux pas, but because the four of them decided to take a taxi together and Paul was late getting his tuxedo back from the tailor. He had to stand around in his underwear while the other three milled about the flat and tried to look interested in a portfolio of etchings awaiting frames. The tailor's driver finally came by at eight, and they made it to La Madeleine by nine.

The first of the decent conversations came when, purely by chance, Max and Django ended up in front of the punch bowl at the same time as the two dancers.

"Who are you?" the first dancer, a slim blonde named Cheri asked. Max took the bait.

"I'm Maximilian Berger. Pleased to meet you."

He stopped there, assuming, correctly, that one of them would ask a follow-up question that might solve the problem of who was supposed to answer, and with what information.

"You sound German," the second dancer, Chloë, said.

"That's because I am," Max replied. "I was a prisoner of war."

"A prisoner!" Chloë said. "How exciting."

"It may seem that way to you," Max began. "But I assure you being captured is not terribly exciting."

"Why didn't you go back to Germany?" Cheri asked.

"I fell in love here."

"With you?" Chloë asked, turning to Django.

"We were lovers in Germany," Django replied. "Not anymore."

"This is getting interesting," Cheri said. "Who are you in love with now?"

"Him."

Max pointed at Marc, who, at that moment, was chatting with Paul in front of one of the fruit platters.

"Hey—" Cheri shouted. "Get over here." Both Paul and Marc looked up. "Your lover wants to speak to you."

The confusion was now universal. Paul and Marc came over and joined Django and Max; each of them thought Chloë was referring to one of the others. Marc grabbed a cup of the punch in order to have something to do with his hands.

"My friend Cheri and I are trying to sort things out," Chloë began. "Max here says you guys are lovers, but I can't figure out what the hell is going on."

Paul, ever the mentor, decided that a helpful explanation was what was most needed at the moment.

"Django and I are partners," he began, putting his arm around his friend as if he was demonstrating the meaning of the word to a school-aged child. "But he and Max were together before that. They've been friends since they were little boys."

"They still look a lot like little boys to me," Cheri said. She turned to Max. "You're cute."

"Thanks."

"And now Max is with Marc," Paul said. "Marc and I are doctors at the American Hospital."

"You're cute, too," Cheri said, looking at Marc. "And a doctor, to boot. *Tant pis*. I could use a few more like you at home."

"And where is home, if not Paris?"

"I was born in Grand Island, Nebraska," Cheri replied. "But I wouldn't be caught dead there now. I like it here."

"Do you have a boyfriend?" Marc asked, turning to Chloë.

"Who, me?" she replied. "I like women."

"I had a boyfriend," Cheri said. "He was British. I met him at Pick's. We had a fabulous month together, and then he left me for another American girl."

"Those Americans," Paul said.

"Don't blame me," Marc said.

"Marc's having an affair with Aurélie Laprix, too," Paul added, thinking he was being helpful in the extreme.

"Who's she?" Chloë asked.

"Your hostess," Django said. "You mean you haven't met her yet?"

"Not formally. Was she the one who took our coats? I thought she was the maid," Cheri said. She turned to Marc. "You're awfully ecumenical for an American. So you like girls <u>and</u> boys?"

"Seems that way," Marc replied.

"Do I have a chance, then?"

"Not tonight. But I wouldn't want to say forever."

"You're cheeky," Cheri said, reaching up on her tiptoes to kiss Marc lightly on his forehead. "Come by Pick's some night. We can foxtrot together and see what happens."

"I'll do that."

By ten o'clock, the buffet had started to be picked over, the champagne buckets needed refreshing, and the band lowered the tempo just enough to inspire an intimate tango or two. Gabrielle kept trying to shake things up by grouping people in mismatched combinations, but there was only so much she could do. The guests experimented with mingling, and then, like captive moons, retreated into small groups orbiting their hosts.

There were other decent conversations springing up around the room and across the evening. At one point, Daphne and Gabrielle found a quiet corner behind a statue of Napoléon and had the chance to reminisce about a shared passionate weekend in Rome before the war, and the courtesan and Pierre discovered they held a common interest in bisexual women. The two deputies stuck to each other's sides like Tweedledum and Tweedledee, and the fact that they looked like twins, with equally ill-fitting suits and matching handlebar mustaches, made them stick out in the crowd.

Django and Max used the safety of the surroundings to act friendly with each other for the first time since their break-up. The long and winding path of their years together allowed them to reconfigure their relationship in a way neither of them had expected.

"How have you been, Maxie?" Django asked.

"I am feeling much better, thanks. This is some party, eh?"

"Happiness and freedom," Django said. "A harbinger of the future."

"Do you think much of your future, Django?"

"I do."

"Are you sorry I am not a part of it?"

Django wasn't sure how to answer Max's question. He had thought Max had moved on, but now he wondered if there was some unquenched longing that was flaring up again in the soft embers of the evening.

"We might be together again someday, Maxie," he replied. "I am still very fond of you. We walked the same path together for many years. But paths change, and end. No one knows what the future may bring, but I'm not lonely now—and you don't seem to be, either."

"*Eines Tages. Die Zukunft,*" Max said, reverting to their

common language for the moment, as if speaking the words in German might bring him back to childhood. "You mention 'someday' and 'the future' with such speculation. After everything we've been through, I was hoping for a little certainty."

"You can be certain that we will always be friends."

"...even if I'm not your lover anymore?"

"Oh, Maxie," Django said. "You will always be my first love, and no one can ever take your place in my heart."

The most dramatic incident of the evening occurred right after midnight. A shoe flew down from the second-floor landing and ended up planted toe-first in the pâté. Everyone thought a fight had broken out, and with it the hope that there was some tidbit worth taking home to gossip about, but it turned out only to be an act of frustration from Daphne. She had grown tired of trying to balance herself on a pair of Chanel heels and was switching to the flats she stored in her handbag. One of the uncomfortable shoes took a dislike to the edge of the carpet and made a suicidal leap in the direction of the nearest silver bowl. The crowd applauded as if they had witnessed an overtime goal at a football match.

Finally, around two in the morning, Aurélie yawned, and the guests took her cue and began collecting their things. Django shook hands with one of the twin deputies, and Paul wondered if a separate peace was being negotiated. Cheri kissed Max on the lips, an act either born out of curiosity or desperation, and Chloë did the same with Gabrielle, with greater success: Gabrielle promised to come watch her dance at Pick's the next week.

Pierre had spent most of the second half of the evening asleep in a very comfortable chair in the library; he came out to say good night to his guests and then retreated up the grand staircase to further his well-deserved rest. The removal of the host was the final bell of the evening and had the likely intended effect of leaving Paul and Django, and Marc and Max, and Gabrielle as the last guests.

"Success, success," Aurélie said, embracing each of them as if they had all just finished acting in a play. And indeed, in a way each of them understood to be true, they had. For a coterie of six who had, at one point or another, carnal knowledge of each other in a moderately alarming number of combinations, theirs was a pleasantly undramatic evening, which—one could suppose—is a kind of drama by itself. There were no arguments, no flirtations (except, perhaps, with the two dancing girls), and no jealous slights. Even Max and Django smiled at each other as they stood together in the hall. Gabrielle was almost disappointed.

"Good night, Aurélie," Paul said, taking Django's arm.

"Thank you for coming, Paul," she said. "Django." Then, she turned to Marc:

"You are left to make the most ambiguous of farewells," she began. "You can leave with Max or stay here with me. Or I could leave with you and Max."

"Or I could leave Max here with you and go with Paul and Django."

"What would Max do with me?" Aurélie asked.

"He and Gabrielle could stay up and play whist," Paul said. "You could go and say goodnight to your husband."

"The only way to put an end to this is with a full stop," Aurélie said. "All of you, go. We can talk more tomorrow."

"If that is what you want, my dear," Gabrielle said. "After all, you are our hostess."

"I play by the house rules," Aurélie said. "Pierre hates to be woken up by unfamiliar voices or the sound of dishes being washed...or smashed."

"Good night."

That was Marc.

"Good night."

Gabrielle called a cab, kissed Aurélie goodnight, and made her way back to the Place Vendôme by three. When she went up, the stillness and silence of her flat startled her; she felt as if a heavy curtain had been draped over her body.

Usually, good parties stimulated her; she'd stay up reading, or fix herself a nightcap. Tonight it took nearly every ounce of energy she had left to pull off the chiffon and the cotton and put on her green silk pajamas. Her barge of a bed never felt so high off the ground, or so soft for sleep.

The following morning, Gabrielle took her breakfast with an unusually larger portion of fate. In recalling last night's party, she saw her affair with Aurélie in a new light. In their twelve years together, Gabrielle had weathered Aurélie's infatuations with both men and women; their sheer number mitigated against any lasting consequences, and after each affair, Aurélie's love for Gabrielle had sprung back into shape, like a comfortable pillow.

But something was different about her relationship with Marcus Greenspan, and the events of the previous evening had helped her to draw a line under what it was. The difference was far more than the fact of his being American, or, for that matter, Jewish—Gabrielle seemed to recall Aurélie's past infatuation with other young men had included some who were one or the other. And it had nothing to do with possessiveness: Max seemed proof that Marc was uninterested in making his love for Aurélie exclusive. Marc's love was also completely different from the love Aurélie depended upon from Pierre, something safe and full of the kind of affection raised up by mutual respect.

If she had to come up with a word for it, Gabrielle's fears about what Aurélie and Marc were doing had something to do with fraternité—it means the same thing in English, but the French word has a little more of love in it. Gabrielle was used to Aurélie taking lovers the way an undisciplined child grabs at toys, but with Marc she was patient and solicitous. It felt like a stop halfway between power and abandon and thus very secure, and it was this abnormal sense of incipient security that worried Gabrielle the most.

Gabrielle had always stood in for the most stable piece of Aurélie Laprix's puzzle of a life, the part that interlocked with all the rest and held them all together. Pierre was the diplomat, keeping the ship of state that was their household above reproach and on all the necessary guest lists; the other lovers—men and women—served as holidays or, if the metaphor was to be continued, unserious military diversions, easily smoothed over by talk or cocktails or just the passing of time.

But Marc was proving to be neither a diplomat nor a diversion, and this was what upset the balance. His behavior at the party put proof to this theory: he now looked like he belonged, as comfortable in Aurélie's surroundings as the furniture.

In the past, whenever Gabrielle was upset with something Aurélie did, her usual medicine was a shopping spree or a flirtatious night out, but in light of the revelation of Marc's semi-permanence, both of these solutions felt like pouring petrol on the fire; they would only serve to strengthen Aurélie's need for Marc's abounding faith. She didn't like playing this game, but it was underway, and she had to figure out the new rules if she had a chance at winning.

The road ahead might be difficult, but Gabrielle felt she had no choice at the moment but to follow it and see where it led.

XII

Django

Django was with Paul at a café on the boulevard du Chateau in Montparnasse. The coffee was getting cold. They had been sitting silently together for a few minutes, and then Django said:

"I think I need to go home."

Django didn't intend to make his announcement sound so dramatic; when he thought about how to talk about Colmar and his future with Paul that morning, he felt it was the beginning of a plan and not the end of an adventure. But as he spoke the words, they sounded final and solitary.

"I knew you wanted to go back sooner or later," Paul began. "But I kept hoping for later."

"What can I do here?" Django asked. "I've been in Paris for almost nine months now, and all I've accomplished is that I've improved my English. I wasn't trained for anything except fighting, and I wasn't even good at that. My papers say I was born in Germany, and no amount of begging for work here is going to make anyone think of me as anything other than a mercenary trying to take away their chance for a job."

"Shouldn't you speak about this with Max?"

"I'm not bound to him anymore," Django replied. "And whatever he wants to do, I'm sure he'd rather talk about it with Marc Greenspan than with me."

"You grew up together. You were close once."

"In time, I suppose, we might be again. But I have to seek my own journey's end now."

"I'd be glad to help you find work here, if you'd like me to," Paul said. "But to be honest, my future is as fuzzy as yours. I'm not sure what my function will be at the hospital once they finish reorganizing it. I know your heart belongs to Alsace. But I was also hoping a small piece of it might belong to me."

"And where is your heart taking you?" Django asked.

"I thought about London," Paul said. "I could start out fresh there. But if you came with me, we might go to Ireland. That way, we'd both be outcasts. The Irish would hate me more than you because I was British."

"But your work at the hospital…"

"I love Paris as much as anyone, but there won't be wounded soldiers needing my care forever."

"I can't ask you to give your job up for me," Django said.

"You don't need to ask," Paul replied. "Now that I think of it, Ireland sounds like a good idea."

"Yes, I suppose it's one way we could stay together. A British doctor and a German soldier in Dublin would be equally exotic. But it still doesn't answer the question about what I can do to help."

The sun was rising and forming long shadows, and the air held that particular early summer warmth that imbues all cities, especially old cities like Paris, with a happy feeling of life worth living.

"I know what I can do," Paul said. "I could love you. After that, everything else will fall into place like the pieces of a puzzle."

"I adore my family, and my heart will always be at home in Colmar," Django said. As he spoke, he heard the tone he recognized in his voice—it was what he heard when he contemplated his life with Max—of love diverging like a fork in a stream, and of directions and choices. "But perhaps you are correct. If we succeed in loving each other, we will have put down roots, and every other branch of my past will hold grow with it."

"I could go to Colmar with you, if you wish."

"I have a hard time picturing you and my mother in the kitchen together, frying up the bacon."

"And I think the picture is charming. But we're getting ahead of ourselves, aren't we?"

"Maybe yes, and maybe no," Django replied. "I'm not certain I'm ready for the future quite yet."

Paul called for fresh coffee.

"Ready or not, here it comes."

Django Bernhardt was correct when he said that he was trained for nothing but soldiering. When he thought about it, alone in the room that he once shared with Max Berger, he understood that had hitched his life to an idea—something about a home and a hearth and a friend—but the idea was stillborn when it tried to emerge into the world. He and Max had been running side by side for a great, long while, but when he stopped to look up, nothing of what he had imagined was there. Surviving the war might be a gift, but when it was over, Django opened the beautiful box that had been placed before him and discovered to his surprise that it was empty.

As Django's story with Max was ending, it was a natural thing for him to reminisce and think back to the beginning. Not that his life was anywhere near to running out; after all, he was only twenty-two years old. But his past was almost entirely filled with memories of Maximilian Berger, and if he was going to find any way of going on without him, he'd have to follow the trail with his finger, like tracing a route on a map, and see if what he had been to Max could in any way inform what he could be to Paul.

There was a reason Django was still drawn to Colmar. His parents were both teachers there, and when he was a small boy the only example he had of how life is to be lived was as a model of instruction: one person shows, the other one does. When, at the age of ten, he and Max began attending the same school, he taught his friend; it was the only way he knew how to behave.

If Max wanted to be a miller when he was older, Django was going to show him how to cut wood, and if Max wanted to be a sailor, Django would teach him to trim a sail. The outskirts of Colmar in those days were unpopulated and inviting, and the two best friends would spend their hours of free time together building little forts along the streams or hunting for acorns and bugs up and down the lightly worn paths, all to underline their generally assumed joint purpose.

Unfortunately for the times in which they grew up, and in a place in a corner of Europe which for the previous decades had served as a perennial battleground, the only available means of escape for the modestly educated sons of working-class fathers were in the Kaiser's army. Django and Max were both seventeen years old when Germany declared war.

Up until that moment, the boys had always thought of themselves as Alsatian, a separate breed that belonged to no country despite the fact that they spoke German and their papers said they were German citizens. Like most of their peers, neither Django nor Max felt any great desire to defend an empire to which they had almost no access, but thirty marks a week was more than they could make doing anything in Colmar. They enlisted.

Along the way, almost as if it were preordained, the two young men strengthened the bonds of their love. This was transparent enough in the company of men, although soon after enlisting they discovered how they felt about each other wasn't strictly necessary to disguise, and—with death all around them—there was no value in waiting for the right time and place to act upon it. A kiss in the woods would no longer suffice.

The consummation of their affair occurred on a quiet night when Django and Max's unit were at ease; the company wandered into an abandoned village just outside of Arles and nestled in an empty barn there. It was a harrowed but also peaceful place. Django and Max found a bed in an isolated stall in a corner of the barn; it was January and cold, and there were no blankets to be found. They ditched their gear and huddled for warmth.

Max put his arms around Django, and Django felt as if every magnetic field in the universe had been pulling him towards this moment. He took Max's hand and placed it on his stomach and encouraged him explore his body. Max kissed Django's lips, and in the burgeoning warmth generated by their bodies they made love. Then, as if blessed and protected by what they had done, they fell asleep in each other's arms. When they awoke the next morning, they understood that something inside the two young men's minds had clicked them together like couplers on a train.

Fate could have done anything with Django Bernhardt and Maximilian Berger. It could have placed them in separate units; it could have turned one man into a naval crewman and the other into fodder for an infantry unit. Had fate been particularly cruel or just arbitrary, it could have killed one man and spared the other.

None of these things happened; the two friends served side by side, in the same unit and in battle after battle, on and off for more than four years. Then, just weeks before the Central Powers collapsed in an undifferentiated heap and sued for peace, Max took three bullets in his leg. He and Django were captured, and their war was over. Colmar—now handed over to the French like a ransomed bauble—remained very far away, as in a dream.

Paris in the late autumn of 1918 was not a likely place for romance, especially if you were an injured German soldier. Max was in grave danger in the American Hospital. In between his prayers for his friend's survival, Django was selling everything he and Max could find just to pay the rent on their flat and buy a carrot or two to keep himself from starving. The cogs in their paddlewheel had worn out, and the gears were not turning properly anymore.

When Django went to visit Max in the hospital, Max seemed uncertain what to say, and Django couldn't find the words to militate against him. Their conversations trailed off, unsatisfactory and directionless. And when Django was alone at home, Max's spirit stayed hidden, like a fog which had obscured the truth and now dissolved to reveal an unrelenting sun. It turned out that devotion was enough to drive them forward together upon troubled waters, but it was not enough to keep their love buoyant when all the circumstances that supported them—their common upbringing and the comradery of war—had drained away.

Django loved Max, but the glow of their adolescent attraction had worn away as the glamour of war faded and was replaced by the lure of being exiled in a new land. Paris was young again, and Django grew younger with it. Convincing himself that the end had come, he asked Max to leave. He made his heart as unyielding as stone because he knew if it opened it even a crack it would crumble.

Max imagined the split-up was temporary; Django was less convinced of this. This void in their feelings created enough space for new and attractive elements to filter in and form a new shape, like magnetic filaments on a metal surface. And that was the attitude they carried along with them when they started out on their affairs—Max in the arms of his doctor, Marcus Greenspan, and Django in bed with Paul Cordette, Marc's colleague. It was something neither of them had once imagined possible, and now it was not only possible, but true.

Django wasn't sure what he was going to do about Paul. When Paul threw out the idea about Ireland that morning, Django thought of it as a lark, but as often is the case with larks, a possibility that started out as fun quickly evolved into something resembling a quest. When he first considered it, Django thought of Ireland as a foreign land as distant as Russia and just as indecipherable.

But after Paul told Django that he found himself staring at the empty beds in the ward and using his spare time to check the prices and schedules for ferries across the English Channel and the Irish Sea, Django began to change his attitude. He wondered if he needed to refresh his paperwork and he bought a second-hand German-English dictionary at a stall on the Seine. Only incidentally, he also found himself thinking about Max and Marc.

One way to solve this unbalanced equation was to force a conclusion: Django could run away with Paul in secret and remove himself from the possibility of being under Max's influence. This seemed wildly romantic, and just a little bit unfair; his inbred sense of honor prevented him from acting in such a precipitate manner, and, anyway, he'd had enough of secrets all his life.

Arranging a grand conference of sorts, with all the interested parties drinking very good beer and toasting to each other's success, felt straight out of a boudoir comedy, complete with the happy ending. The only problem was that one wrong turn could just as easily turn it into a domestic tragedy. It was best to steer this ship clear of any shoals. Instead, Django continued to drift.

Django met Paul for dinner at a favorite restaurant of theirs, an inexpensive place in Chaillot run by an Alsatian couple. The familiar comfort of the dishes calmed Django; this made him more open than usual to importuning. He hoped that his own anxiety about the decision to come might be hidden behind the strong beer and good cuts of beef.

"I know you've been eager for us to move in together," Paul began. "I am, too. But first, I need to ask you a couple of important questions."

"Do I need to order something to drink first?" Django asked. "Or will I be able to answer sober?"

"Do you still love Max?"

"I would call that an important question," Django said. "Are my only possible answers 'yes' or 'no'?"

"Maybe."

Django laughed.

"Of course, I love Max," he said. "But what you mean is, do I love him enough to be unfaithful to you?"

"That wasn't precisely what I was trying to get at," Paul said. "But I suppose you got the gist of it correct."

"Can we move on to the next important question?" Django asked. "I think I know what it is, and my answer to the first one might be conditioned by how I feel about second."

"Would you come with me to Ireland?"

"Yes."

"Yes, but…"

"Was there a 'but'?" Django asked.

"I sensed one."

"I'm trying to put 'Max' and 'Ireland' together in the same thought process. I'd like to do what's best for all of us, but since I don't know how the others feel about it, I'm finding the answer hard to sort. Have you and Marc had any chance at all to talk about what he plans to do with himself, or, for that matter, with Max?"

"Not yet," Paul replied. "I'd like to make plans with you before making plans with Marc and Max."

"You are assuming Marc has included Max in his own plans."

"That's true. And then there's Aurélie."

"I guess she comes under the heading 'Marc's plans'," Django said. "Perhaps we need to hire a consultant."

"It's not that complicated. I trust love," Paul said. "And I hope you will, too."

"Love is one thing," Django said. "But will you be able to find work in Dublin? I suppose Irish doctors will have priority."

"One of my colleagues at the American Hospital did his internship at Mater Misericordia there," Paul said. "I could speak to him about it. I may have to train for a new specialty, but the people there—especially the Catholics—need all the help they can get. Something might turn up for me."

"What could I do?"

"That's up to you. Whatever makes you happy, I suppose."

"Living with you would make me happy."

"I meant the world is your oyster."

"That's a dreadful expression, Paul," Django said. "But I

like oysters, and I hear they're ripe for the picking in Dublin Bay. I say 'let's go'."

Paul smiled.

"Now the world is my oyster, too."

Django went ahead with getting ready for the move. He gave his two weeks' notice to his landlord in the middle of May, and he wrote to his mother and his father back in Colmar, filling them in on all his adventures since the Armistice and promising them he'd send them the money for a trip to Ireland just as soon as he was settled. He left out saying anything about Max, who—of course—they knew, or just what it was, exactly, that he was doing with Paul, but that was because he still hadn't figured out what to say to himself.

There was still one large step left to be taken for this plan to work: Django had to present it to Max as a fait accompli. He knew himself too well to leave any hidden coils that might be sprung at the last moment to block his plan. If he went into battle unarmed his defenses would be stripped and his cause would be lost; he'd be unable to resist falling for Max all over again. He wondered if it might be better for Marc to come with Max when they met, a human buffer against all the friction, but that smacked of cowardice, and he hadn't been brave all through the war only to give in to shirking his responsibilities in the end.

The end—or at least the beginning of it—came on an otherwise ordinary Thursday evening in the neutral territory of a café on the rue de Sèvres.

"Hi, Maxie," Django said. He pulled out Max's chair and embraced him and kissed him on both cheeks, just as he had done a hundred times before and in a hundred different places.

"It's good to see you," Django said.

"Likewise."

"You look good."

"And you look like you have always looked," Max said. "Hungry."

Django smiled. Max had always commented that his friend was too thin, and the comment sparked a pang of memory from their time together, of meals dashed down between adventures in Black Forest and kisses snuck under the eaves of Saint-Mathieu. The small talk continued through the drinks—two aperitifs—and the ordering: a bacon and tomato sandwich for Max, a slice of quiche Lorraine for Django. Django felt like a boxer about to lean in for a decisive punch; Max was likely innocent of Django's circling.

"I'd like to finally try to settle our plans," Django said.

"It's interesting that you refer to them as 'our plans'," Max said. "I hadn't realized we were planning anything together, at least not anymore."

"Our plans may be separate, Max, but our lives shouldn't be. No matter where I go, or what you do, I will always be thinking of you and care about you."

"By this, shall I infer that you are going somewhere?"

"I meant that in a general sort of way, but, as a matter of fact, Paul and I are going somewhere. To Ireland."

"Ireland?" Max asked. "That's out of the blue."

"And that's precisely why we chose it. There's too much of the past clinging to Colmar or Paris or London. We both wish to live together in a new place, without anyone to judge us."

"At least you're not going to America," Max said. "That would be beyond the pale, and certainly beyond my budget."

"America may be beyond the pale, Max, but you are sleeping with an American. He may have homing instincts of his own."

"I don't think Marc has any plans to go back to America," Max said. "In fact, America is coming to us. His fiancé is due to disembark in Le Havre tomorrow."

"That's a fresh form of complication," Django said. "How are you going to deal with it?"

"I'm leaving that up to Marc."

"And what does Marc want to do about it?" Django asked.

"He's torn. Wouldn't you be? The two of them have been

buddies forever. It's wild. Sarah and Marc were just like you and me, and look how we turned out."

"Yes, but there's still love between us," Django said. "There may be some left between them, too."

"You've caused me to think about leftover love," Max said. "And I'm not as torn up about your leaving and going to Ireland as I thought I might be. I guess we have a different kind of bond. And, of course, the world looks at Marc and Sarah differently. Their engagement was public, and the break will be, too. Nothing about how we loved each other was or ever could be conventional."

"I still wish you good luck."

"Oh, I don't know if luck will help," Max said. "I'm on firm ground with Marc. I just have to stick to my guns."

"Guns, my dear Maxie, are what got us into this mess in the first place. Dublin is not so very far away from Paris. If you stay here with Marc, I will see you again. Maybe the four of us could meet once we all get settled. Who knows?—you may end up in Ireland."

"That's an idyllic picture," Max said. "And a hopeful one."

"I still love you in my way, Maxie."

"That's kind of you."

"I don't want our friendship to end."

"I assure you, that won't…that can't happen," Max said. "Not after everything…"

Max let the sentence drift off. 'Everything' can mean a lot of different things, and the weight of that uncertainty stopped the conversation in its tracks.

"I'll get this," Max said as the garçon placed the bill on the table.

"*Nächstes Mal*," Django added.

"Yes, next time."

At home that night, Django started to pack. Paul had booked them passage on the ferry out of Caen. The trip was still two weeks away and Django didn't have that much to take with him, but once the forward motion had begun he didn't feel much of a need to linger. All of his clothes fit into one suitcase.

Almost everything else except for his new suit and changes of underwear could be left behind; he'd only want the winter coat he bought with money he made selling contraband cigarettes when he first arrived in Paris and Max was still in hospital. Ownership of the framed postcard of Colmar needed to be decided, along with the little whirligig that stood on the bedstand. Life, like the blades of that toy, keeps revolving, and Django's memory of his time with Max would need to revolve with it, no matter where or how they lived.

Just before Django fell asleep, he counted his lovers. It wasn't quite as neutral and calming as counting sheep, but it fit his mood of moving on that was so dominating his thoughts. There were few enough of them to recall precisely. First, there was a boy in Colmar—he couldn't recall his name—who found Django's body fascinating and spent a good part of a summer exploring it. Then there were the two men from his unit during the war—Sam, a Jewish kid from Berlin who gave Django literally his first taste of circumcision, and one junior officer named Heinrich who actually liked giving up his command in bed. But all through these men and boys, and others whose names and even actions had faded over the years but who still remained visible enough to count, there was Max: Max the first, Max the eternal, Max the lost.

Max persisted even in Django's dreams, dreams that now included the cold spray of the Irish Sea under a summer sun, incomprehensible accents, and automobiles driving on the wrong side of the road. Even while picturing Paul driving the car or imagining a home perhaps a block or two away from the hospital where Paul would work, or the shop somewhere along the Liffey where Django would sell penny postcards and souvenirs, there was Max, like a figure in a white cloud, looking down and blessing him.

Django wished he could fall asleep and wake up in two weeks.

XIII

Sarah

Sarah Gold wasn't sure how to tell Marc that she had fallen in love with Herschel Milner. Slipping the news into a letter—especially the latest letter, the one that ended up crossing with Marc's in the mail—seemed unchivalrous. A telegram would just be cruel; it had the right amount of dramatic power, but Sarah always had a hard time figuring out the time difference between Louisville and Paris, and a cable informing your fiancé you are breaking things off might be ill-received at any hour but even worse at midnight.

In the end, her best solution was the most extravagant one—to sail to Paris and deliver the news in person. It took time and it was expensive, but Sarah felt that Marc's patience and devotion across the years required a concomitant effort on her part; the ending of things would thus contain an appropriate amount of drama and Marc's reaction could be parsed in real time. It was the consideration of that reaction, as well as the sequence of events that had caused the break in the first place, that consumed Sarah's thoughts for the ten days crossing on the La Touraine.

Sarah thought it ironic that she had known Herschel almost as long as she had known Marc. Both boys' families belonged to the same synagogue as the Golds, and the two young men were close enough to Sarah in age to cross her path in school and at prayer. She still had strong memories of sitting in the sanctuary for Herschel's Bar Mitzvah and for Marc's confirmation.

Sarah drifted into Marc's orbit not because she loved him more than Herschel, but that their common interests in history and languages meant there was more to talk about over dates; Herschel was just as polite (he brought her bouquets of roses; Marc preferred boxes of chocolates) but less assertive. The steps in Marc's direction were tentative, but they were steps, and in the spring of 1914, she accepted Marc's proposal and started to wear his engagement ring.

When Marc asked for Sarah's permission to volunteer for the American Ambulance Field Service, she granted it, all the while wishing she could refuse. She knew her wish to keep Marc at home was selfish, but she kept her disappointment and frustration to herself. Sarah was tethered to Marc like a child with a balloon; there was always the possibility that their separation would be like letting go.

On top of that Sarah thought Marc seemed just a tad too eager to leave. She wondered if there was something more than patriotism or the opportunity for experience driving his decision. They hesitated to talk about it in earnest and then suddenly it was too late; Marc shipped out that summer. There had been nothing but letters ever since.

During the war, Herschel Milner accepted the role of beneficent friend: he escorted Sarah to events that required chaperoning and made sure she was not lonely. Sarah was not secretive about Herschel's attention; she wrote to Marc about him and he encouraged her in his replies. He could hardly act possessive from a distance of three thousand miles.

Sarah, on her part, went along with the wedding plans, despite her worry that if she was changing as the years apart went by Marc was changing, too. It was this incremental sense of change that led her to slowly stop thinking of Marcus Greenspan as her intended. The connection she had once reserved for him was now much better fitted to Herschel. Young Mr. Milner wasn't a doctor, but business accounting was no discipline for slouches, and he was handsome in a different way from Marc, with a beaming, crooked smile and bristly black hair that always looked like it needed brushing.

All through the years that Marc was overseas, but especially in the last year, Sarah sensed the need to reconsider her decision. Should she stick with Marc and hope for the best, or press her luck with Herschel and see what might happen? This left the unlikely but still fraught possibility of being caught between two stools and leaving her to face an early—and possibly not temporary—old maidenhood.

Sarah started to imagine Marcus Greenspan and Herschel Milner as two boys playing on a seesaw, each aggressively trying to shake the other one loose. She was unwilling to be a mere spectator to their game, and longed to be the one playing, but she knew of no way to resolve the dilemma. Sarah even started to wonder what might happen if, God forbid, Marc died. That would be the least blameful solution.

Time provided clarity to her vision and allowed for a resolution. Sometime that winter, Sarah Gold realized the seesaw ride was over: Herschel's counterweight had won. She went with Herschel to a garden party at Churchill Downs, and there she told him that, when the chance arose, she would break off her engagement to Marc. Herschel, true to form, said he could wait. Now the chance had come.

The first thing Sarah did when she arrived in Paris was go to the American Hospital and look up Marc. The confusion over timing—the slowness of the ship, the fear of missed messages—left her without a surefire way of knowing when or where they might meet. She had his address, of course, but hanging around on the boulevard du Château while hoping to spot him coming in or out his building seemed inappropriate and just possibly might raise suspicions.

Sarah thought she had given Marc the name of her hotel—the Majestic, a few blocks from the Arc du Triomphe—but asking him to meet her there, even by telephone, felt like a business arrangement. In the end, she could think of nothing to do but visit his place of work and hope for the best.

Sarah found a taxi lingering at the dock. The driver dropped her steamer trunk off at the hotel and took her to the hospital. She left her card with a note at the desk and took a seat in the waiting room. It turned out that the first person to check in there was Paul Cordette. He spotted the card, read the note, and rushed over to greet the overdressed, slightly tired-looking American girl sitting on the visitor's bench.

"Miss Gold," Paul began, taking her hands in his and kissing her lightly on the cheek. "I am Dr. Paul Cordette, Dr. Greenspan's colleague. He's told me so much about you. It's a pleasure to meet you."

Sarah bowed.

"Please, come and wait in my office. I'll go and fetch Marc."

Paul escorted Sarah down the hall. He unlocked the door to his office, took her portmanteau, and asked her to wait in a chair in the outer room.

"I'll be right back."

Sarah felt the next few minutes might just be the longest of her life. She half-expected the young man who would come back in with Dr. Cordette would be unrecognizable. Had Marc changed his appearance? Did he now sport a mustache? Had his hair grown in? For a brief moment, she forgot what he looked like; the old photograph she kept on her nightstand—taken at his graduation from Harvard all those years ago—was certainly out of date, and furthermore, she had replaced it with one of Herschel months ago.

"Sarah."

And there Marc stood, exactly the same, as if he had just walked off the dock in New York and into an office suite in Paris. The first thing Sarah felt was disappointment: he hadn't changed, after all.

"Marcus."

They embraced.

Marc told Sarah his shift ended at six o'clock; he made plans to pick her up at the Majestic at seven. He'd make a reservation at a place he liked on avenue Kleber only a few blocks from the hotel. They could catch up then. Sarah knew she had perfected the art of dissembling from a distance; the time had come to test her skills at it in the flesh.

Sarah changed into something blue at the hotel, remembering it was Marc's favorite color. She thought that this might help her to temper her news with nostalgia for their past which, after all, would soon be all they would share. As she put on the dress, she recalled Marc's embrace in Paul's office; it felt reticent, even considering Paul's presence, and she wondered if this feeling was Marc's or her own. She was nervous as she went down in the elevator, and fanned herself in the lobby while waiting, even though, for May, it was not that warm.

"Good evening, my darling."

Marc burst out from behind a column. He was wearing a crimson-colored suit with a gold and red striped tie. Sarah was glad she had put on her good jewels; their meal might be casual but she didn't care to look out of place, and the news to come needed a heightened sense of eloquence.

"Hello, Marc," she said. "You look handsome."

"And you look lovely, as ever," he replied. "Let's walk."

The restaurant Marc had chosen was a ten-minute stroll away; they went arm in arm and passed the time in silence. Sarah was certain there was some sort of speech ready to pour out of her beau, but she had no idea if it was a renewal of their vows or a confession. She thought, *wouldn't it be fantastic if he was thinking the same thing about me that I was thinking about him? That would make things so much easier.*

Their table was ready when they arrived.

"Well," Marc began, laying the napkin on his lap and unfolding the menu. "How shall we start?"

"Do you mean with the meal or with the rest of our lives?" Sarah said.

"Both begin now," Marc said. "But I suppose our future is the greater topic, despite the quality of the food here."

"Marc." Sarah had no idea how to go on; the pressure of

all that was unspoken between them was starting to become unbearable. She buried her nervousness by deflecting her attention to the food. "What will you have, my dear?"

"The fish is always good, and a white Bordeaux, I think."

"Sounds good to me."

"Marc," she repeated. At that moment, Sarah felt like she would never be able to go any further with this conversation than the constant repetition of her fiancé's name. Just then, the garçon came over. Marc ordered.

"*Deux filets de sole, et la Sémillon, s'il vous plaît.*"

"*Merci.*"

The illusion that Marc was the same as ever lasted all through their reunion at the hospital and part of the way through their first evening, maintained by the crowds and the time needed for adjustment, but once the waiter left and the two of them were fundamentally alone, Sarah sensed that Marc was ready to lift the curtain. It was the moment of equipoise that she was waiting for. She was about to speak, but Marc interceded. He said:

"I should tell you how I've changed."

"I would have expected nothing less."

"I love you, Sarah…"

"Oh, Marc," Sarah said, cutting him off. "I know you too well. Any speech that begins with the words 'I love you' will contain something I don't want to hear. But I'm afraid I have something you don't want to hear, too."

"Tell me," Marc said.

"You first."

"Very well." Marc took a sip of his water. "I am in love with someone else. He's a man I met at the hospital, a former patient. His name is Max, and he was a German prisoner of war."

Marc had rehearsed this very brief speech for a week, ever since he knew he was going to have to deliver it to Sarah in person. The earlier versions of it were full of detailed explanations and apologies and went on for far too long. He even tried to find a way to place Aurélie in the picture, but that made the speech even longer and far more convoluted. In the end, he felt plain reportage—and under-reportage, at that—would work best.

Just then, the wine arrived. Marc tasted; the sommelier poured. Sarah fiddled with her napkin but said nothing.

"Say something, Sarah."

"I am going to marry Herschel Milner."

Sarah took a sip of the wine, as if she had just concluded a kind of blessing. It was Marc's turn to react, but—like his fiancé—he had no words. He sat there, glass in hand, in silence, watching the legs of the wine make their slow descent. Finally, Marc spoke:

"Well, there we have it."

"I'd say you changed, all right," Sarah said. "And so have I."

"Don't be bitter."

"Oh, did I sound that way?" she began. "I'm sorry. I might even laugh. It's all so topsy-turvy. Forgive me, but I feel I have the right to ask. When did you start to prefer men?"

"I always knew it was there," Marc said. "I successfully paid no attention to it. I had no reason to. I loved you. But what changed in me was not my preference for men or women, but what I saw and felt about mankind through all the years of fighting. Forgive me, but after you've seen friends bleed to death and parts of bodies pile up like firewood, you start to revalue what you need to live. I was overwhelmed by the war, but I was overwhelmed by the peace, too. I felt like my old soul was washed out, and a new one flooded in, one filled with a passion for life. Somehow, that passion flowed into my friend. It was practically undetected until it was too late. His name is Max."

The garçon arrived with their food.

"You must love Max very much," Sarah said.

"I do, as you must love Herschel."

"Yes."

"You know I love you, too, Sarah," Marc began. "I always

have. But my love for you was devotional—almost literally, like a religion. We grew up together. I wanted more than anything in the world to protect you, to help you raise our children, to grow old together…"

"…without ever wondering where the passion was," Sarah said. "I'm afraid we both played by the rules, and the war changed the rules."

"Tell me about Herschel."

"He knows we were engaged," Sarah said. "He is an honorable man, and he is waiting to hear from me after I talk with you."

"Do you feel relieved?" Marc asked.

"Yes, and no. I still feel linked to you. I'd like to be your best friend. We deserve that for each other. But best friends should incorporate each other's gossip. You must tell me more about Max."

"He was under my care, having survived three bullet wounds. I was at sea with the war winding down. We crossed paths at our moments of greatest need."

"I hope you and Max can go on."

"I hope we can go on, too. Time froze after I heard you were coming. I'm not sure what he and I will do next."

"Does Max want to go to America?"

"You should ask, do I?" Marc replied. "America must have changed too, and I'm not sure if it's the right place for me anymore. Dr. Cordette—Paul—is going to Ireland."

"Ireland?"

"He has a lover. His name is Django. Django used to be Max's boyfriend. Django and Max grew up together in Alsace, and they came to Paris after Max was wounded."

"Your tale is getting more interesting by the minute," Sarah said. "I feel like I've walked into a Colette novel."

Marc laughed. The mention of one of their favorite French writers, and one who specialized in the varieties of love, gave him the entrée he needed to expand the landscape of the conversation to its full borders.

"I guess I should also tell you about Aurélie Laprix," Marc said.

"What? You're not done with your Parisian escapades? Marcus Greenspan, you are beginning to sound like some sort of rake."

"It's not quite like that, Sarah. I met Aurélie before I met Max. She's married. And while the two of us have kept company, she also has a lover, a Slavic lady named Gabrielle."

"My goodness! You've outdone Colette, I must say. You must find my American provincialism quite boring."

"Don't be like that, Sarah," Marc said. "I'm not telling you all this to impress you. My life here is complicated, and I'm trying to tell you about it as plainly as I can. It's purely the truth, and I certainly owe you a full explanation."

"Let's recap for our readers at home," Sarah began. "You wandered away from your engagement to a charming Kentucky debutante to begin simultaneous affairs with a German soldier and a married French lady. The German soldier also has, or had, a lover, as did—or does—the French lady. You must be exhausted. I certainly am, just listening to you."

"Please forgive me, Sarah," Marc pleaded. "I didn't plan for any of this."

"And that just might be the war's best epitaph," Sarah said. "*I didn't plan for any of this.* I can see it written on every soldier's tombstone and as a motto for every general's memoirs."

"It does sound that way, doesn't it?"

"I suppose America and bohemianism don't mix," Sarah said.

"It's not that. It's just that...well, with so much happening, and with the world changing around me, I felt this enormous pressure to keep up. I've been so busy at work, helping Paul, and learning to love Aurélie and Max that I haven't had the time to think about where I want to go next, or even if I want to go anywhere at all."

"Can't Max stay in Paris?"

"He might. He grew up in Colmar. He could go there, or to Ireland with Paul."

"And what, if anything, do you plan to do about your affair with Aurélie?" Sarah asked.

"Aurélie seems wonderfully happy being married to Pierre Laprix and in love with Gabrielle Sternberk," Marc replied. "So for her, there's much less of a reason for me to hang around. I think I ended up being more or less a fillip to her experience of the peace. As for me, I suppose the actual *dénouement* depends on what Max decides to do."

Marc stopped to punctuate his thoughts with another sip of his wine. The daylight started to fade, and the view outside the restaurant's windows began to fall into shadow. It was like a curtain being dropped at the end of an eventful act in a play. The drama of Marc's and Sarah's confessions faded, and what remained was a sort of settled landscape; now that the two of them knew where the sightlines were located and what obstacles—or lack of obstacles—had been placed in their path, they both felt more secure in making their way forward.

"I'm sorry you had to cross the Atlantic to find all this out," Marc said.

"I suppose I could have invited Herschel to come with me," Sarah said. "Then the two of us could have played at being characters in a Henry James novel, witnesses to a continent's willfulness."

"You could have done that from Kentucky."

"Nonsense. I wanted to cross the Atlantic. I had to tell you about me and Herschel."

"How ironic!—while we were engaged an ocean kept us apart, but as soon as we were reunited, without any space or time between us, we separated. Our balloons are untethered."

The garçon came by to take their plates and ask about dessert and coffee.

"I'll have the lemon tart," Sarah said.

"*Une tarte au citron et deux cafés, s'il vous plaît.*" Marc twirled his fork. "How long will you stay?"

"I had planned on two weeks," Sarah replied. "The La Touraine sails back on July 4th."

"There's a lot we can do together between now and then."

"Do you think I should meet Max and Aurélie?"

"It might be unusual, but I know they would be delighted to meet you," Marc answered. "Django, too. You must know they've all heard so much about you."

"But I am very different from the person you told them about."

"And I am very different from the person who sailed to war from America," Marc said. "So for all of us—even you and me—it is as if we are meeting for the first time."

"I like that," Sarah said. "The old world and the new world switching places. Everything is new, and so are we."

The garçon came back with their tart and a coffee urn. Sarah's mood brightened visibly. It was as if, once the storm clouds hanging over her head had cleared, and now that she knew Marc was not stuck with her under their symbolic umbrella, they might resume the friendship they had cultivated so well in the past.

"What shall we do now?" Marc asked. He was asking about their future, but Sarah responded as if he had asked about the present.

"Let's go back to the Majestic and dance."

There was dancing nightly in the hotel ballroom. Sarah had spotted a notice to that effect when she first checked in, and it prompted a memory—she and Marc at a cotillion in Lexington, Kentucky in the summer of 1912.

They were twenty-one years old, and it was their first formal ball. Both of them had other dates, on and off, over the years, but the seriousness of the event frightened them into a form of shared formality. Sarah was resplendent in a glittering orange gown; Marc rented a tuxedo and brought her a bouquet of two dozen white roses. They hired a coach to take them to the hall, danced a dozen dances, sampled both the alcoholic and non-alcoholic punches, and rode back to Louisville in a cloud of peaceful accommodation. It was the first major step in the direction of their engagement.

The Majestic ballroom was not quite cotillion-level, but the band was good. Sarah thought Marc looked happy to have made his way through Aurélie and Max with her, although she didn't wish at the moment to think too hard about what a final sorting would look like—that would require definitive choices, and Marc didn't look ready for it yet. Sarah was relieved to realize that she didn't have to break Marc's heart.

The band struck up 'After You're Gone.' Sarah took Marc's hand and led him out to the dance floor. There was a deliberate poignancy to their steps, as if the two of them were not only enjoying their time together but dancing their last dance. As Sarah felt Marc place his hand gently around her waist, she wished so much that he was her brother and not her fiancé. That would suit him so much better. She closed her eyes and tried to imagine herself years ago and very far away. *We should have always been just friends,* Sarah thought... *uncomplicated and honest. There's so much unravelling yet to be done...*

Around two A.M., the musicians put their instruments away and the bartender shouted for last call.

"I will always love you, Marcus," Sarah said. They were sitting together side by side at a table, as if there was something still to see going on at the bandstand.

"I'm glad we can still be friends," Marc said. "There is a special feeling between us."

"A special feeling," Sarah whispered. She was getting sleepy now, and she put her head down on Marc's shoulder.

"Our motto," Marc said.

Marc escorted Sarah upstairs to her room; on the threshold, he kissed her goodnight.

XIV

Aurélie

Once Sarah had grasped the lay of the land—getting a grip on Marc's on again, off again (but mostly off) affair with Aurélie and his mostly on-again affair with Max—she was determined to at least get in the spirit of things and try to gain a better understanding of it. One by one, she was going to single out all of Marc's new friends and, like a sponge, try to absorb from them all there was to learn about her former fiancé's life in Paris.

The evening after the dancing was spent touring with Marc and Max. In order to increase her sense of being *au courant*, Sarah wore a felt cloche hat she bought that afternoon and put on some very shiny jewelry and a pair of comfortable but chic shoes. The three of them walked up the Champs-Elysées, shared steaks and frites at a café across the street from Sarah's hotel and had drinks in the lobby until one. Sarah felt very modern in the presence of the two men, as if she was one of the models in an advertisement in Paris Vogue and they were her business managers.

The next morning, she and Marc had brunch with Aurélie and Pierre in the dining room of their Madeleine townhouse. It was a simple affair of croissants, brie, and coffee, if anything conducted amidst Fragonard landscapes and Houdon busts could be described as 'simple'. Pierre spent most of the time on the telephone, and Sarah came to the not quite unreasonable conclusion that he functioned more as his wife's social secretary than as her husband. The following day, Sarah and Marc went to have lunch with Aurélie and Gabrielle; it was from that successful outing that the idea of a daring night out was born.

The original plan for the evening was for Marc and Sarah to go to someplace risqué with Aurélie and Gabrielle, a nightclub with nude dancers or with an opium den in the basement. The problem was that from the moment Sarah arrived in Paris Marc had spent all of his free time with her; this defeated the purpose of weaning his ex-fiancé from his affection and made any of their possible demi-monde destinations less than outré. It's hard to be dissolute when you're chaperoned, so Marc bowed out. Max was (he jokingly said) beginning to feel neglected.

Then Gabrielle claimed she had a headache, a not improbable result from being up for twenty-four hours straight, and in the end for the grand night out Aurélie and Sarah were reduced to a couple. Madame Laprix met Sarah in front of the Majestic at nine—warning her in advance to eat something light and wear a pants suit—and they took a taxi up to a bar in Montmartre.

Sarah understood the reason for the request for pants when she got a good look at what Aurélie was wearing: a sheer black chiffon party dress with a gold and white blouse and pearls. Apparently, they were going to enact a play, one in which an older, sophisticated woman served as Vergil to an innocent, boyish Dante. Sarah was a bit apprehensive, but also a little charmed; after she first found out the truth about Marc and Max, she feared she was going to spend her time in Paris as a third wheel, and it was nice to be singled out. It didn't matter to her how.

"Am I safe here?"

Sarah intended her question to be ironic, but Aurélie had only known her for three days, after all, and she wasn't sure if the girl was serious or not.

"Of course," Aurélie replied. "They're lesbians, not vampires."

The two women were standing along the bar at La Violette.

There were a few open seats in the back of the room, but Aurélie wished for her companion to be, in her words, 'where the action is'. The action, as far as Sarah could see, constituted posses of women, some dressed in top hats and tails, others in gowns, roaming the periphery of the room like hungry wolves. It was a parody of the courting rituals she witnessed time and again in the lounge of the Seelbach Hotel in downtown Louisville.

"I knew these kinds of places existed," Sarah began, as they watched two heavy-set girls in matching tuxedoes pass them by on the way to the dance floor. "But I couldn't imagine what they looked like, or how the people who went there behaved."

"You were never curious?" Aurélie asked.

"Me? No. I had a girlfriend in high school who asked if she could kiss me. It was the asking that I found strange. All my friends kissed each other all the time, and it never meant anything. I suppose it's different with boys. I never spoke to Marcus about it, and I probably never will, now."

"But the two of you can still be friends?"

"I think, in retrospect, we always were friends," Sarah replied. "The idea of marriage was put in front of us like a normal next step after going to parties and picnics together for ten years. It's different in America."

"That's an understatement. I think if I had to live in America, I would get arrested within an hour. Most of the things I like to do are illegal in all forty-eight states."

"You're exaggerating," Sarah said. "Life might be boring in Kentucky, but there are big cities where people are much less judgmental. You might try it sometime."

"Are you hoping Marc goes back to America?"

"I was," Sarah said. "For two and a half years, that was my fondest hope and dream. I fed off of it, and I practically needed nothing else. I had fooled myself into thinking if it happened all my wishes would come true. And all the while, I was repeating with Herschel what I had done with Marc—waiting, hoping. Then I understood that Herschel was there, and Marc was not, and—well, I stopped waiting and hoping."

Their glasses were empty. Aurélie ordered two more champagne cocktails.

"I feel that way about Gabrielle," Aurélie began. "I was like a child with a diorama. I kept moving all the figures around and around until there was no one but her in the center."

"Is Marc one of your diorama figures?"

"Oh, I didn't mean to sound flippant. I have a very special relationship with Marc. I think I offered him something that he needed at the time that we met."

"But you don't think he needs you anymore?"

"It wasn't me that he needed, but what I had."

"And what was that?"

"I don't know," Aurélie said. "I can try to put it in words, but it will sound insipid—wisdom, patience... the kind of things a young man often lacks and an older woman often provides."

"You aren't that much older, are you?"

"My dear Sarah, age is found not only in numbers of years but in varieties of experience."

"Marc often wrote to me about how the war was changing him," Sarah said. "But I always thought he was referring to the carnage and the fear. I guess it turned out to be something else entirely."

"I think where you might be wrong is that you think Marc changed. I don't think people really change. I think the world changes, and we respond to it. It's all about fate and opportunity. Max might have been assigned another ward, or not injured at all, and he and Marc would never have met."

"Max," Sarah said, as if by saying his name she was invoking a spell, something to calm the turbulent waters of her time in Paris and all the figures in her life floating in it.

"To boyfriends and girlfriends," Aurélie said, lifting her glass for a toast.

"I'll drink to that," Sarah said. "Let's have another."

They spent the rest of the evening watching the parade pass by, never caring if the chance might be their last.

One night, about midway through Sarah's visit, Marc made plans with Aurélie to spend the night together. The tone of Marc's voice on the telephone and the precipitousness of his request led Aurélie to think of this meeting as a prelude to – or perhaps a literal expression of—a farewell.

The two of them drifted through drinks at a bar on the boulevard Saint-Germain and a light supper of bread, oysters, and sauterne at a café opposite the Musée du Cluny. Aurélie thought about all the questions she wanted to ask of Marc and of the answers she expected to hear, but nothing of the subject she most feared was spoken. Marc did not mention Max, or Sarah; instead, he complemented her on her dress and touched her shoulders with the tentativeness of a suitor. It was if he was beginning with her anew.

Aurélie suggested a visit to the bar at the Hotel Albe. It was the site of their first assignation, and it held a special place in her memory—a reservoir of peace and freedom into which they could immerse their bodies. The classical columns of the portico, the gilt-leaf decorations on the ceiling in the lobby, and the plush velvet rugs on the stairs all spoke of nostalgia for a world free from quotidian care. After hastily drunk cocktails, Marc suggested they take a room. When they entered it, Aurélie felt like a curtain was being raised on some grand drama; there was a hush in the air, which made her reticent to speak.

Even their lovemaking, so familiar and yet still so foreign—diversified by age, experience, and purpose—was nearly silent. Aurélie undressed and pulled the soft silk sheet over her breasts. Marc stood at the foot of the bed with his shirt unbuttoned; if there had been a witness, he or she would have thought he was an artist arranging a pose.

Then Marc took off the rest of his clothes and climbed into the bed to embrace Aurélie. They clung closely to each other as if for warmth, even though it was June. Aurélie bit Marc's ear, gently, like a cat. He held her breasts and kissed her softly on her neck. Something had changed about the way they were touching each other, but it was difficult for Aurélie to formulate what it was in a way that made sense; it was as if the closer they drew together, the further they fell apart.

Afterwards, Marc opened the bottle of Veuve Clicquot that he brought up from the bar and they sat side by side on the bed, draped in nothing but the bedsheet, drinking. If he had his way, the two of them might have basked in the afterglow and stayed in a state of suspended animation forever, but Aurélie's mind was heavy with thought. She felt the need to unburden it.

"Have you decided where you and Max will go?"

"You make several assumptions with that sentence, Aury," Marc said. "You assume that Max and I will go somewhere, and not stay here. That it will be Max who I stay with, and—for that matter—that I have made any kind of a decision at all."

"What are you waiting for? Sarah has made her choice, and I have made mine."

"You chose Gabrielle."

"It's not a beauty contest, Marc," Aurélie said. "There's no need to declare a winner. You always knew, right from the start, that I did not want to leave Pierre, and that I would always love Gabrielle. We only never decided to set terms for our time together, but I think, like for Sarah, and Paul and Django, that the moment has come."

"You make it sound like we signed a contract."

"It was an open-ended one, I suppose, but it was a contract none the less. We decided to love each other until something or someone forced us to stop."

"No one is forcing me to do anything," Marc said. He was beginning to feel at a disadvantage.

"And that's good. One never wishes to let an affair last long enough to require force to end it…or to continue it, for that matter. Anyway, it is fruitless for us to argue about it. It is clear as day to me that you are in love with Max, and you and Max should decide on your future together."

"You asked me if I had made a decision about Max, but it sounds to me like you have made the decision for me."

Aurélie laughed.

"Sometimes, my dear, you are such a silly boy! I wouldn't have said a word about it if it weren't completely obvious. Can't you see? Max loves you more than words can ever say, and you revel in it because you know, *cor cordium*, that you feel the same way about him."

"Who knows?" Marc said. "I might go with Paul and Django to Ireland, and Max could come with me. Or we could stay in Paris. For all I know, Max may want to go back to Colmar, and I'll have to go back to America. I certainly haven't talked to Max about it. In fact, I've tried very hard not to think about it at all. I feel like I've never had the chance."

"You deserve that chance," Aurélie said. "More than anything in the world, and borne upon my most sincere wishes, Marc, you deserve that chance."

The talk, such as it was, was over, but there was still half a bottle of the Veuve Clicquot. Good champagne should never go to waste.

All the clashing pieces of Aurélie Laprix's life had brought her to an impasse, as if she had been driving merrily along an alpine road and a landslide had landed in her path. Her months with Marc blinded her to the reality of the new world rising from the ashes of the old.

Before Marc, and all through the war, Aurélie clung to her routines—breakfast with Pierre, a chat with the staff, volunteer work until lunch, visits to whatever stores were open and had goods worth buying, then a languorous tea or dinner chez Sternberk, sometimes spending the night, sometimes in carriage back to the Madeleine. There were diversions in the form of brief affairs, but it was part of a pattern which now seemed as seen through a distant mirror.

When Aurélie met Marc, every bit of their time together seemed to be like a burrowing into a core. She carved her week into parcels divided by encounters with her newly beloved. It was bliss, and a novelty, but—like all kinds of bliss, and all variety of novelties—the charm began to wear off over time.

Aurélie was much too happy about it to want it to end, but at the same time, she knew that the ebb and flow that was Marc was like a river, eternal but equally undefined and uncontained. There must come a moment in all love affairs when it is time to step out of the flow.

Aurélie's life with Gabrielle Beauchamps was different. If Marc was a river, Gabrielle was the earth, solid, held in place by the insurmountable pull of gravity. The equation was as simple as that. It took first her falling in love with Marcus Greenspan, and then meeting Paul and Django, and finally seeing what had happened between Marc and Max for Aurélie to understand that her life needed to finally revolve around a single axis.

She'd spent twenty years splitting her allegiance—Pierre, male lovers, female lovers…how could they ever add up to anything resembling a direction? Pierre, she supposed, came the closest of all; he had several of the necessary qualities—patience, dedication, position—but lacked the most important one of all, passion.

On the day after she and Marc broke things off, she asked Pierre if they could meet in the parlor after breakfast. This was not an unusual request, one Aurélie might make on any ordinary morning. Pierre assumed his wife merely needed to ask for some money or wanted to parry him with questions about a new painting for the dining room or a china pattern that she liked. He was surprised, and mildly put off, when she asked him for a divorce.

"I thought we were content together," Pierre said. He had carried his coffee cup from the breakfast table to the parlor and was annoyed to discover it was nearly empty. "Would you mind if I ring for more coffee while we talk?"

Aurélie, on her part, was just as bothered that Pierre had managed to somehow equate her request for a divorce with his need for more coffee, as if her ultimatum was just another small interruption in the day's routine. It was just the sort of thing that prompted her to take such an extreme action in the first place.

"We were content," Aurélie said. "I was content. I've spent over a dozen years with you. But if I learned anything from the lessons of war, it's that being content is not all there is to life. The rhythm of our lives changed, and when I tried to restore it, I found the pieces had broken in my hands. I wanted to scream."

"Don't scream, my dear," Pierre said. "The walls are not that thick and you may disturb the servants."

"You may mock me all you wish," Aurélie said. "I want to live with Gabrielle Sternberk, finally free of my obligations to you."

"I always thought you enjoyed your obligations."

"I don't mean the balls, Pierre. I mean my social standing. It has grown worthless to me. I do not wish to play Madame Laprix anymore."

"I hadn't known it was an act."

"Now you're being arch. It's all an act, and the time has come for me to write my own play."

"I assume you will not need a settlement," Pierre said, switching—seemingly in an instant—from the spurned husband to the sharp-eyed businessman. "Gabrielle Sternberk will provide."

"Gabrielle and I can provide for each other, Pierre," Aurélie said. "Or did you forget I came with my own dowry?"

"I have not forgotten about the Beauchamps fortune. But your union with Gabrielle will have no legal standing. What will you do when you turn fifty and grey? Or when she leaves you for some ambassador's daughter?"

"I will take that risk."

"You jump without a safety net, like an acrobat in the circus."

"Life is a circus, Pierre. If you have learned anything, you must know that. I am on a tightwire, and you must allow me to be free to walk across the wire, or to fall."

XV

Max

It was Max's idea that the whole gang should go to Pick's for a farewell fling—he and Marc with Sarah, Paul and Django, Aurélie and Gabrielle. Max even asked Aurélie to invite Pierre in order to have an even number. Pierre was willing to come provided he could make an early evening of it and wouldn't have to dress up in anything too outlandish. Aurélie reassured Pierre that Pick's was more like a visit to a menagerie than an invitation to a costume ball, and the party was set.

Paul told Pick that something special was happening that evening, and a table for eight near the band was reserved. This turned out to be a fortuitous bit of planning, for their evening at Pick's ended up, quite accidentally, being held on the same June day that the Treaty of Versailles was signed. All of Paris was celebrating out on the streets and in the clubs, and people without reservations, already half-inebriated, were lining up in front of Pick's waiting to get in.

The four young men shared a taxi from Batignolles to Montmartre. Max was in high spirits, and not only because of his happy mood; he and Marc had started drinking early, with daiquiris in a bar on the boulevard du Château before heading over to Paul's place. Marc brushed off his tuxedo—he hadn't worn it since the reception at the Institut Pasteur—and Max wore one of Marc's suits that he had tailored so the cuffs wouldn't drape and the sleeves didn't hang down over his fists. When they stopped to pick up Paul and Django, Max couldn't help but notice that Django had made a point of wearing a tight pair of gray linen trousers to accentuate his body and a top hat that was guaranteed to make him the tallest man in the room.

The four of them were amongst the first to arrive at the club; they wandered over to their table to wait, and while they waited, they took in the view. The crowd was both familiar and unusual: Paul spotted two drag queens whom he knew by name—Fantômas and Phoebe. Apropos his criminal namesake, Fantômas was distinguished by a black mask, augmented, in this case, by a feathered headdress and enough toile to strangle himself. Phoebe, being the relatively more demure of the pair, was decked out from tip to toe in a spangled black velvet cat suit with a plunging neckline.

The unusual element was a greater proportion of soldiers in uniform, although from a distance it was hard to tell if they were actual soldiers or women dressed as men. Pick, as always, greeted every guest and ran from table to table making certain the glasses were full and the plates were groaning. In honor of *la victoire*, everything was on the house.

Pierre and Aurélie came in next; Pierre insisted they arrive together, a simple act of coordination that would help to tamp down the gossip that was certain to spread as the evening wore on; he even hired a coach to make sure their timing was noticed. This assuaged just enough of his sense of propriety to allow him to almost immediately relax and shelter himself in the comfort of a glass of aged Bordeaux.

Gabrielle was solicitous of Sarah's position and arranged in advance for her to come over to her place on the rue Sainte-Honoré for some last-minute touch ups; they could go over to the club together and avoiding giving anyone the impression that Sarah was unaccompanied. Mademoiselle Sternberk also made certain they would arrive last and thus make the most dramatic entrance.

Gabrielle arrived wearing a full-length gold satin gown with a white chrysanthemum in her jet-black hair, and Sarah had on something from Printemps that Gaby bought for her the week before and was fitted by the best tailor in Chaillot. All action in the room seemed to stop as the two of them made their way, very slowly, from the front door down to their table where the rest of the guests gave them the clubgoer's equivalent of a standing ovation.

"Isn't this too much?" Paul shouted as they took their seats. He needed to shout because the band struck up 'Oui, Oui, Marie' at that very moment.

"Let's get settled and then order," Pierre said. As the oldest person at the table, he instinctively installed himself as the host. He picked up the menu, but it was so tall it blocked his view.

"I'm not sure what you need to do to settle, darling," Aurélie said. "Do you want to do check my wrap?"

"No, my dear. It was just a figure of speech."

Marc had been counting Max's drinks, with a wary eye on preventing him from getting drunk too early in the evening. He wondered if perhaps Django's presence was making his friend nervous. Max, not being so encumbered by any need to keep track of what he was drinking and too far along to care what anyone thought, signaled the waiter almost before he had sat down.

"A pitcher of daiquiris, *s'il vous plaît*," he shouted.

"That was quick," Gabrielle said.

"It's a start," Max answered.

"Max…"

Marc realized that their party was a little too large to steer; the best he could hope for was to keep Max from wandering too far off the straightaway. But before he could think of any action that might help him to do this, Sarah took his elbow.

"We're in France," she said. "I don't need to wait for someone to ask for my card. Let's dance."

Sarah pulled Marc onto the dance floor. 'Oui, Oui, Marie' had ended, and the band was now playing 'I'm Always Chasing Rainbows'. The slow pace and lowered volume allowed the two of them to talk.

"I'm sorry to be so brusque, but I knew if I waited any longer to dance with you, I'd spend half the evening trying to cut in," she said.

"I don't mind," Marc said. "I always liked dancing with you."

"Ah, yes—cotillion after cotillion, I remember," Sarah said. "And this may be my last chance. When are you and Max leaving for Ireland?"

"A week from Thursday. Paul and Django are going over first to scout for lodgings, and then Paul is supposed to send me a telegram with the when and where of it."

"That doesn't sound like much of a plan," Sarah said.

"It's enough of one for now. When is your crossing?"

"July 4th. I depart from Cherbourg. I'll be sad."

"Sad? Why?"

"I've known it's the end of things for us," Sarah replied. "My time here has been a kind of summing up, but putting a stop to it just makes me feel sad."

"Let's not be sad tonight," Marc said. "Let's celebrate being older and wiser."

"You might be older," Sarah said. "I'm merely wiser."

When 'I'm Always Chasing Rainbows' ended, the band broke out 'The Tiger Rag'. Pairs of dancers stampeded to the floor and further conversation became impossible.

The whole of the evening progressed in tiny traces. The couples took turns on the dance floor, with the pairings practically changing with each new song. Paul danced two dances with Django, and then one with Sarah and another with, of all people, Marc. Pierre chaperoned Aurélie to the floor for the first verse and chorus of 'I Love A Piano' and then bowed out for first Marc and then Gabrielle. Sarah even danced one dance with Aurélie, although they spent most of the time gossiping about the other women's dresses.

Pierre gave his regrets and grabbed his hat at eleven, as he had planned to do all along. He knew his presence was the one least required, and so his farewells were brief and polite. Aurélie grew hungry just before midnight and put in an order for the table—some cucumber sandwiches, a plate of cornichons and gruyère, and a fruit platter. The role of host more or less devolved to Marc; he seemed to end up in the middle of every conversation and the focus of nearly every invitation to dance.

At one point, in the middle of changing partners, Marc realized this might be his last opportunity, at least for a while, to hold Aurélie in his arms, and this realization filled him with an unexpected ache. His decision to move forward with Max seemed straightforward when considered in the plain light of day—always the best light for making big decisions—but in the glow of the evening and mellow with drink, something about his choice felt unfinished, as if the next slide in the projector was clicking into place before he had really taken the time to study the present one. When their song ended, Marc and Aurélie parted as any ordinary dance couple would, but to Marc it felt like something more permanent. He tried to dwell on it, but the hubbub of the room roared back and the second hand swept on.

Meanwhile, Max was getting increasingly drunk. He told dirty jokes that apparently sounded better in the original German, and he kept pulling on Marc's sleeve like an overeager ten-year-old.

At one point, the band struck up 'La Cumparsita'. Max got up to dance with Django; this gave Paul and Marc their best chance to take the pulse of the night, and the situation, and their plans for their lives going forward. They were, for the moment, the only couple at the table. Gabrielle had grabbed Sarah and was introducing her to the black jazz singer on her break.

"This has been like a dream," Paul said.

Paul's statement was undirected, and Marc wasn't sure how to respond.

"Do you remember the day we met?" Paul continued. "I think it was in the summer of '17. You had just been reassigned from Lille, and I thought you were as cute as hell. But I had an overflow of wounded men to tend to. I think I shouted at you before I even learned your name."

"It was a hard time," Marc said. "I forgave you."

"I couldn't imagine a day of peace, let alone a lifetime of happiness, and now here we are."

"Unless Django sweeps Max off his feet again," Marc said. "Look at them now."

"Oh, I wouldn't worry about that. You're in luck—four best friends."

"Is that what we are?" Marc asked.

"Four best friends, and two pairs of lovers."

"I suppose if the circle is to be complete, you and I would have to go to bed together."

"Don't imagine I haven't thought about it," Paul said.

"Really? Well, I'm sorry to disappoint you, but Max and I vowed to be faithful to each other."

"Did you ask for a minister, or a rabbi?"

"Don't be droll, Paul. A vow made in the heart is just as worthy as one made on an altar."

"I'm glad to hear it, truly I am."

"Do you love Django?" Marc asked.

"Yes."

"Then we will be solid."

"As solid as any Irish peat bog can be."

Max and Django came back. Max looked flushed, and Marc wondered if it was the drink, Django's influence, or merely the fast tempo of the song.

"Who taught Max to dance?" Django said. "Last I looked, he couldn't manage a two-step, let alone a tango."

"The last time you saw me dance, Django, I was sixteen years old, and it was an off-kilter polka with a farmer's daughter. You must know I've earned eons of sophistication since then."

"I'm jealous," Paul said.

"You'll get your chance later," Django said. "We can dance together until dawn."

"Is it last call yet?" Max asked. "I'm thirsty."

"I think you've had enough to drink tonight," Marc said.

"Thank you, *mutter*."

Max stood up and gave Marc a friendly shove. The shove evolved into an embrace. Marc pulled Max into his arms and kissed him, for longer than Max had expected, on the lips.

"Is that to stop me from drinking?" Max asked.

"No. Here's some water."

"I've changed my mind," Max said. "I'm not thirsty for a drink, even of water. I want more of you."

"I am mostly water, after all," Marc said.

"There's oceans of it, between the four of us," Paul added.

Just then, the girls returned.

"Do we have time for one last dance?" Sarah asked. "I don't want this night to end."

"I don't either," Marc said. "Shall we dance?"

Marc led Sarah out to the dance floor. The band played 'Musetta's Waltz,' their usual closing encore. Sarah guided Marc's hands around her waist. She closed her eyes. Marc kissed her gently on the forehead.

"You deserve all this and more, Sarah," he said. He spoke softly over the music, but Sarah heard him.

"So do you, Marcus. I wish for happiness at last for all of us."

The clock struck two.

It would have been happiness at last for everyone, but the morning after the party at Picks', Max claimed to be exhausted and stayed in bed. Marc put it down to a hangover and left his friend alone while he went to work. The day was filled with the usual rounds and one or two patients who needed extra attention, but all in all Marc thought he had finally crossed the highest hill on the roller coaster that had been his life for the past three years. It would be an easy ride from here on.

Overnight, however, Max developed a high fever and he started to complain of a tingling in his legs. First thing the next morning, Marc decided to take Max to the hospital. Paul Cordette took one look at Max and checked him in to a free bed in the nearly empty ward.

Marc was supposed to do that morning's rounds, but Paul found another doctor to spell him and Marc had the chance to stick to Max's side. Each time Max woke up, Marc brought him glasses of water and wiped the sweat off his brow, but the afternoon came with no change in Max's condition. Marc noted, with the sense of a premonition, that Max was now back in the same ward where they had met, and very nearly the same bed.

Around three, Marc's hunger overtook his worry. He had forgotten to eat all day. He walked out to the boulevard du Château and had a cheese sandwich and a cup of coffee. The sandwich tasted bitter and the coffee made his head hurt. For a moment, he thought the way he felt was a residual effect from his overeating and heavy drinking, but he had never been sick from partying before. There must have been another reason.

When Marc returned to the ward, Paul met him at the door.

"Max has gone into shock," he said. Paul put his arm around Marc; it was what Paul did all the time with friends and family when he knew a patient was going to die. "I think he is suffering from blood poisoning."

Max had been brought down to the operating theater; the surgeon there thought that something had gone wrong with the bullet left in Max's knee, and they were going to open up the wound and investigate. Paul sat with Marc on a bench outside the room where the doctor and the nurses were working. They waited there for an hour.

The surgeon came out.

"We were too late," he said. "The bullet's copper casing broke and the lead got into his blood. The infection caused a severe sepsis. I'm so sorry. Maximilian Berger is dead."

There is always a moment when really bad news arrives and it feels like the world has stopped revolving, a faint fading of the sense of sight and a loss of balance, as if, in a dream, one were falling from a great height. Marc felt this way and said nothing, preoccupied at first with trying to stay on his feet. He thought that if he collapsed, he might never rise again.

It was Paul who spoke first, a wordless cry that translated into a picture of inexpressible grief. Marc recovered from his dizziness, but his next thoughts were of displacement, as if he was Paul and not himself, and he was letting Paul suffer for him. Strange, he had lived with death and feared it, and even watched it happen over and over again during all his years of service during the war, but he had never completely understood how final it could be until he heard the news about Max.

Marc's next thought was to believe the doctor had made a mistake. It couldn't be Max who had died, but another patient; could they check his chart, please, make certain the name on it was correct? Then, when he realized he was hearing the truth, he wanted to die with Max; at least that way they would still be in the same place, wherever that might be. Finally, once that feeling had passed, Marc listened to himself, and all he could hear was the sound of the heavy beating of his heart. He was alive, after all.

The moment had come, and now it was gone—completely gone, over. Nothing more will happen to Max. Marc realized then that he had already known Max was dead—it happened when he had his premonition and was underlined for him when Paul held him in his arms. There was solace in his knowing that all through those last moments he was with Max in spirit. They were together one last time.

Paul made the arrangements to have Max's body shipped back to Colmar so his parents could bury him in their local cemetery. For Marc, the whole city of Paris, which only two days ago had been seized with celebration, now seemed shrouded in mourning.

Marc wanted to be the one to tell Django. He called him up, and the three of them—Paul, Marc, and Django—met at a cafe in Batignolles, a block away from Paul's flat.

"I've got very bad news," Marc said. "Max is dead."

"*Mein Gott!*" Django shouted. He put both hands on the

table, as if to keep himself from falling. "What happened?"

"Blood poisoning," Paul said. "From the bullet. It's rare, but it happens."

Django said nothing more at first. He stirred the spoon in his coffee and wished he could do nothing else forever. Then he looked directly into Marc's eyes.

"So the war killed him, after all," Django said. "I'm sorry, Marc."

"We all are," Marc replied. "God is very cruel."

"Is it right to blame God?" Django asked.

For the first time since the ordeal began, Marc cried, gently flowing tears, more of resignation than of grief. Paul took Marc's hands and held them in his own.

"You should still come to Ireland with us," he said. "You'll be very lonely on your own."

"I don't know what I want to do," Marc said. "All I can think about is Max."

"You don't have to decide anything yet," Paul said.

"Before Max goes to Colmar, we should have some sort of ceremony," Marc added. "Is there a Lutheran church in Paris?"

"Django and I can help you figure everything out."

"Thank you."

"I should tell Aurélie and Gabrielle," Marc said. "And, of course, Sarah."

"Yes, you should."

Marc didn't want their conversation to end. He preferred letting it drift away, for when his friends left the café and went back to their lives, Max's presence in his life might dissolve with it. The thought of that was, for the moment, unbearable.

XVI

Marc

"How are you holding up, Marcus?"

Sarah asked Marc this question as she was clearing the plates from the breakfast table. Taking pity on her friend after his loss, Sarah had spent the night in Marc's flat; it was a chaste evening, but still something she would never dare to do or even think of doing while they both lived in Louisville. Marc had been brooding; of course, an easy consequence of the events of the past few days.

"I don't think I can go to Ireland with Paul and Django anymore," Marc replied. "But I'm sure I can't live in Louisville, either, much as I'd love your company. Every place I've ever been feels haunted to me now. I need to go to some place where I don't have any memories."

"Memories aren't bad, Marc," Sarah said. "Right now, they're painful, but they say time heals all wounds. Look at us. We share pleasant memories. You and I have learned how to be friends. We can go on that way, don't you think?"

"Yes, but you're alive, Sarah. You and I can grow old remembering and changing as we remember. Max is dead, and there's nothing I can do about my memories of him but repeat them in my mind over and over again. I think if I was in a city that Max never saw, or away from the people Max knew, it would be easier for me."

"That sounds very lonely."

"I think I need to live alone," Marc said. "Start again in a place where I know no one."

"Where could you go?"

"I thought about New York. It's full of opportunities, and as a Jewish doctor, I'm certain to fit right in."

"Why don't you sail back to America with me, then?" Sarah asked. "I'd like the company, and your trip wouldn't be so lonely."

"You wouldn't mind?"

"How could I? We never quarreled. I still love you, in my way. I'm certain Herschel will understand once he hears the whole story. If that's what you want to do, let me know, and I'll help you make the arrangements. I'll telegram Herschel and he can come up to meet us in New York."

"You were always the practical one, Sarah. I could use a little practicality."

Sarah got up to carry the plates to the kitchen.

"Au contraire, Marcus. I think you should allow yourself an extra measure of impracticality right now."

That afternoon, Marc went to see Paul and Django in Batignolles.

"I'm going to hang my shingle in Manhattan," he said. "I've thought a bit about it, and it's the best thing for me to do. I think I'd like to be in a city where I can't stay stuck in the past…no memories."

"And no friends," Paul added. "I don't like to think of you all by yourself."

"But who do you know in Dublin?" Marc asked. "You'll be all by yourself, too."

"Paul and I will have each other," Django said. "And if you were there, you'd have us with you."

"I love both of you," Marc replied. "And I certainly will miss your company. But I'd be like a man missing a limb. How could I look at the two of you and not be reminded of the empty space next to me—the space that belonged to Max?"

"When will you go?"

"Sarah's arranging a berth for me on the La Touraine. We'll travel together."

"There's a bitter irony," Paul said. "You were engaged on your way over, and she's engaged on her way back, but no longer to each other."

"It'll be a chance for she and I to talk."

"What more is there to talk about?" Django asked.

"Oh, if you pardon my pun, I believe we have oceans to discuss. I know her finding out about Max and me was a shock, but I think she's at least come to understand why it happened. After all, we were friends before we were a couple, and she's practically been by my side since we were kids. I don't put a lot of money on the theories of Dr. Freud, but perhaps an ex-fiancé could help me with my feelings. I need someone to talk to about Max."

"You can talk to us," Paul said.

"I can, but you and I, Paul, and you and Max, Django—that's years of psychoanalysis all by itself."

"Someday, we'll look back on all this and think we were crazy," Django said. He gave a bitter laugh. "The world went mad, and we went mad with it. I think as my English gets better, I'd like to try and write a book about all things I only imagined when I was a boy and how much of that I've already experienced—love, war, and death."

"That's profound," Marc added. "And I'm glad you're able to think about such things. I can't—not yet. Can we talk about something else now? The past is all sorrow to me. Tell me more about your plans."

"I've written to an estate agent in Dublin," Paul said. "He thinks he can get us a flat once I have a letter of employment. We'll stay in a hotel while I look for a job. There are five hospitals in the city alone, and I do speak the language, more or less."

"I'm going to Colmar first," Django said. "I know Max's mother and father. I should be there with them to help with the final arrangements."

"I wish I could be there," Marc said. "I feel like I at least owe that to Max."

"That's true, but Max is beyond the point of repayment,

and although the Bergers might appreciate the fact that you tried to save their son's life, I'm not so sure they would understand how much you loved him."

"You're right, of course."

"But I'll mention you, certainly."

"Thanks."

"Have you arranged a service here?"

"Yes, at the Church of the Redemption in Faubourg-Montmartre, tomorrow at ten," Marc replied. "I know you'll both want to be there. I telephoned Aurélie to give her the news, and I'm going to go and speak to her this afternoon. She'll get in touch with Gabrielle. It'll be very sad, but I think it's necessary."

"Soon, I hope, we'll be free of necessity," Django said. Marc smiled.

"That's a wish worth keeping under my pillow."

Marc arrived at the Laprix townhouse right after lunch. There were two servants running up and down the stairs, and people—likely movers—coming in and out of the rooms.

"Marc…" Aurélie greeted Marc in the portico and kissed him on both cheeks. "I am so sorry. I apologize for the madness. All the events of the past week have triggered a great migration. I've decided to move in with Gabrielle, and Pierre has ordered up an inventory while I pack."

Marc suddenly felt like he had been transformed, in Aurélie's estimation, to another piece of furniture needing relocation— one more item for her inventory. He thought they had parted amicably, but with Aurélie, one never knows.

"This is precipitate," was all Marc could manage to say as a young man swept past them carrying a Chinese vase nearly as tall as he.

"Come into the library," Aurélie said. "It'll be quieter in there."

She led him into the room where about a third of the Laprix's impressive library had been taken from the shelves and stored in wooden crates.

"Where's Pierre?" Marc asked.

"He's down at the Hotel du Ville," she replied. "He ran off straight after wolfing down a sandwich, and he sends his apologies."

"How is he taking your decision?"

"Oh, I think he regrets most of all that he won't have someone to talk to after he finishes with the papers at breakfast. We both are really very independent, and this house—for all its faded glory—was a convenience which outlived its utility. I'm ready to let the ghosts who reside here rest in peace."

"I hope Pierre can come to Max's service," Marc said. "It's tomorrow morning, at the Church of the Redemption."

Aurélie looked up into the skylight, as if she was searching for some sort of redemption up there for herself.

"Gabrielle and I will attend, of course," she said. "I'll talk to Pierre about it, and hopefully he will come, too."

"I'm leaving for New York on Friday," Marc said. He hadn't planned on making his plans sound so dramatic, but as events in the Laprix household seemed to be catapulting over him he felt the necessity to get his news in edgeways before Aurélie crowded him out with a fresh revelation of her own.

"So soon?" she replied. "There will hardly be time for our farewell dinner."

"I didn't know...I hadn't planned on a dinner."

"Is this, then, our goodbye?" she asked. "No dinner, no Hotel Albe?"

"No, Aurélie. It's better this way."

"Better for you, you mean."

"You have Gabrielle to turn to for consolation," Marc said. "I have only the memory of Max."

"You have the memory of me, I hope."

"Yes, I do."

"But it is complete?"

"Complete now, yes."

Aurélie cast her gaze on the half-empty bookshelves. Marc wondered what her next move would be—an angry accusation, a shrug, a lover's sweet importuning. Aurélie surprised him, and perhaps even surprised herself, by doing none of these things. She stood up and wandered over to the other side of the room, searching for a book. When she found it, she pulled it out and handed it to Marc.

"It's the first edition of Goethe's 'Hermann und Dorothea,' published in 1799. It's my gift to you. I want you to have it."

"But isn't it very valuable, Aurélie?"

"It is, but no less valuable than you are to me," she began. "I want you to keep it and think of it as a reminder of all that happened between us, and what happened to you. It's a story of love and war. The German poetry will remind you of Max, and Hermann's love for Dorothea will remind you of me."

"That's very thoughtful of you," Marc said. "You were always so kind."

"The past tense, at last," Aurélie said. "Now, please take it, and put it away before I start to cry."

Marc was touched and also shaken by Aurélie's gift and her reaction when he accepted it. In all the time they were together, he had never seen her cry, and, indeed, he had never imagined a circumstance in which she might be provoked to do so, not even now. When he and Aurélie made love, she was always so assertive, so sure of her place and her role, that the idea that Marc could say or do something that might bring her to tears was unimaginable. Now it had happened.

Marc stood up and crossed the room, took the book from her hand, and kissed her gently on the lips. A single tear fell down Aurélie's cheek.

"I will always remember this moment," Marc said, "And I will think of my love for you when I do, Aurélie."

Aurélie regained her composure.

"You had better, Marcus Greenspan."

The memorial service at the Church of the Redemption was as beautiful as Marc had hoped it would be. There were large bouquets of red geraniums—the most popular flower in

Alsace—on either side of the pulpit, and Max's mahogany casket glowed in the candlelight like a holy shrine. Marc instructed the church's staff to leave the casket closed, not because there was a reason for hiding his body but because, while speaking to Django about it, he felt that it was more important to say goodbye to Max's spirit. The presence of his body was beside the point.

The pastor was told in advance a few brief bits of information about Max's life, but, of course, the most important pieces of it—his love for Django and his love for Marc—had to remain unspoken. Aurélie and Gabrielle were resplendent in black—Aurélie in a linen sheath dress with a single white rose pinned to the collar and Gabrielle in a cotton suit with navy blue velvet trim. Pierre was behind them, fussing with his missal.

Marc sat in front with Paul and Django on one side, and Sarah on the other. At one point, when Marc was fairly sure the congregation was paying its full attention to the pastor's words, he took Django's hand in his and squeezed it. Django smiled.

Marc looked up at the dark grey stones of the vault and wondered if there were any answers to the questions he was asking there. What kind of redemption was promised by the name of this church? What glory lay in death by an ounce of lead, whether in the form of a bullet or a poison of the blood? Marc almost wished Max had died in battle; at least then there would have been a medal waiting for his family when his body was carried home, but such an ending would have precluded Marc ever meeting him and denied Marc the perfect love he experienced and the lessons he had learned from it.

What were these lessons? The eternal student that Marc liked to imagine himself searched for some maxim—pun intended—to pull out of the ashes. Surely, Marc had learned something of the meaning of love, a feeling beyond lust and settling in the stomach as a form of hunger to do better and do right for one special person. That, plus something of human resilience, evidenced by his ability to survive and love after the shock of war and then—seemingly in an instant—face the end of it and still be alive.

There was a moment near the conclusion of the service when the pastor asked for a silent prayer for Max, and Marc found the strength to say to himself everything that he had been unable or unwilling to speak aloud: *I have never loved anyone the way I loved Maximilian Berger.* Surely, it was a love beyond need, beyond lust, not even unique for Max being a man or born out of my pure admiration and respect, although certainly those were qualities contained in it. *No*, Marc thought, *what Max taught me about love is how the need of it can finally show you how to love yourself.*

Marc wished he could bury himself in Aurélie's arms, but he was not simple enough to believe this would save him. He'd had his fill of burials, after all, some—like those at war—literal and others hidden in his mind, with Max the last and most bitter. Memories do dull with the days as time passes, but Marc was suddenly impatient. He needed to face the future alone.

After the service was over, there was just enough time for one final reunion: Aurélie and Gabrielle, Paul and Django, Sarah and Marc (Pierre, as expected, grabbed a taxi in front of the church and sped off with barely a salute). They walked around the corner to a café on the rue Drouot and commandeered a table for six next to the staircase.

The room was crowded and noisy, but something about what they had just been through, and how they were once and would forever be linked by joy and sorrow, led Marc to think that their party was composed of acolytes, removed from the church but still circumscribed in holy communion. Maybe it was just possible for Jews to believe in saints.

As soon as they had been seated, Aurélie ordered steins of German beer for everyone in Max's honor. Marc offered the toast.

"To Max," he said, standing up and raising his glass. "A better soldier and a better man in a better world."

"Aye," Paul cried, as the rest lifted their glasses in salute.

"*Auf weidersehn*, Maxie," Django said.

Just then, the light shifted, and the shaft of a beam opened up on the bench next to where Marc was sitting. It shone brightly on the empty spot next to him, a clear blessing.

"*Danke*," Marc whispered, so softly that no one else could hear him.

The next day it was time to go. Travel is always distracting, and in the bundling up of the trunks and the suitcases and the confusion over fitting in a meal, calling the taxi, and catching the train to Le Havre Marc didn't have the chance to catalogue any of his regrets. It was all happening too fast. There is never really enough time to think about what has been or what might be in the face of a train schedule or a ship's sailing deadline.

The train from Paris to Le Havre left the Gare du Nord at nine; the ride took two and a half hours, just enough time for Marc and Sarah to make a visit to the dining car and for Marc to struggle through the first half of Gide's 'L'Immoraliste'. They slept for the last hour. Then it was time to unload, sign in, stride up the gangway, and find their way through the immense maze of the great French ocean liner.

Marc's and Sarah's berths on the La Touraine were at opposite ends of the same deck; his was as close to hers as could be managed at the last minute. Marc packed a trunk that contained about a quarter of his clothes (the formal wear and most of his suits were to be shipped separately to a storage warehouse near Wall Street) as well as a dozen or so books—including, of course, Aurélie's first edition Goethe.

Max's postcard of the church in Colmar was a parting gift from Django; Marc managed to wedge it in between one of his dress shirts and his shaving kit, an ordinary but still sanctified place. Sarah, as expected, had less to pack—her portmanteau and small trunk sufficed, as she only needed extra room for the few things she bought, or that Aurélie had bought for her, in Paris.

After settling in, Marc and Sarah made plans to meet on the

upper deck to watch the embarkation. The day was warm and foggy, and beyond the smokestacks of the liner and a few masts in the harbor nothing of the land or the sea was visible; it was as if they were floating in space, and, in a bubble of magic, they might be transported from the coast of France to the foot of the Statue of Liberty in a matter of minutes.

Most of the passengers came up top for this ritual, and the rails were thronged with people waving handkerchiefs at the invisible spectators. The two of them walked until they found an unoccupied bench, and they sat there together.

"Are you sad to leave Europe?" Sarah asked.

Marc didn't answer at first. His mind flipped through everything he had a right to feel sad about—the loss of innocence, the dead of war, the last of the oysters and the champagne, saying goodbye to Paul, Django, Aurélie, and, of course, Max—and the weight of it all felt like an anchor holding him fast. But thoughts of sadness are naturally replaced, or at least balanced, by better thoughts, and at that moment, Marc realized that everything that he laid down heavily in the 'sad' column as lost could someday be equally, and just as validly, marked in his memory as 'happy' and found.

Marc thought of the men he and Paul had healed and saved, the hours of work in the surgical wards nearly always ending with shared tears of joy. There was Django's stoic beauty, his survivor's instincts, and his new-found love for Paul. Marc thought of Aurélie—that first, impossibly erotic night in the Hotel Albe, and her enthusiasm for every experience. She could turn a mundane day into an adventure, like a child who thinks everything she sees for the first time is brand-new to the universe.

And then there was Max. When he thought about Max, Marc felt something akin to the pain of an electrical shock; it was as if, with the shroud of fog to finally stop his eyes from seeing everything that was in front of him, he at last had the chance to be alone with his memories of what felt like his one great love.

In his mind's eye, Marc pictured Max's smile, so unimaginably innocent after all that he had been through, and Max's chest, so much like his own that when Marc fell asleep upon it, he felt as safe as if he was wrapped in his own arms. There was Max's kiss, both gentle and assertive, as if to say 'I love you this much, but soon there will be so much more'.

And then there was no more.

"No," Marc finally answered, recalling Sarah's question about missing Europe. He surprised himself with the word. "I am finished being sad. Look at all I've done. Look at all I've learned."

"That's true," Sarah said. "Despite all the death, and all the sickness, you found something beautiful to come out of the ashes. But now that Max is gone, won't you miss all that beauty?"

"Beauty is both effervescent and omnipotent, Sarah," Marc replied. "It is of a moment, like a rose, and eternal, like stone. You might as well ask if I miss the spring, or God."

The whistle blew, and the great engine of the ship was engaged.

"Here we go," Sarah said. "I wish we could see more of the harbor."

"After everything I've been through," Marc said. "I'm glad for the fog. This way, I can imagine everything I'm leaving behind."

"Will you ever come back?"

"Yes, but that will have to wait for another turn of the page. Someday, I'd like to visit Paul and Django in Ireland, and I'd like to go to Colmar and retrace Max's steps."

"You make it sound like a pilgrimage."

"A pilgrimage back to grace, yes."

The ship sailed out into the harbor.

About the Author

Bob Sennett is the author of 'The Music Teacher' (nominated for a Lambda Literary Award for Best Debut Fiction) as well as several books about Hollywood and photography. He loves doing research and spinning stories out of gay history. Bob worked as a librarian and art historian at Harvard University for thirty years. He is now retired and living with his husband in the beautiful city of Prague.

Author photo by Martin Večeřa

Excellent LGBTQ+ fiction by unique, wonderful authors.

Thrillers
Mystery
Romance
Literary
Young Adult
& More

Visit us at
www.spectrum-books.com

Or find us on Instagram
www.instagram.com/spectrumbookpublisher

www.ingramcontent.com/pod-product-compliance
Lightning Source LLC
Chambersburg PA
CBHW010021130526
44590CB00047B/3764